Win By 100

Praise for *Win By 100*

"*Win By 100* is a must-read for anyone who dares to grow. Whether you're a coach, leader, or simply someone hungry for change, this book lays out a clear blueprint for transformation. Through the MADE System—Motivation, Assessment, Declaration, Execution—Holloway combines hard-won personal wisdom with battle-tested strategies from the field. The result? A real, honest, and effective guide to winning in life and leadership. Readers will walk away more self-aware, more resilient, and more powerful."

- **Skip Bates, ACC**, Executive Coach, Clear Rock Consulting

"The MADE man is passionate about unpacking MADE in his latest book, *Win By 100*. Loaded with personal stories, leadership insights, and pragmatic, usable solutions, TJ Holloway will both lead and challenge you to embrace MADE—and to win in every area of life."

- **Dr. Sam Chand**, Global Leadership Consultant and Author of *Leadership Pain*

"At its essence, the delightful surprise in this insightful work is its empowerment. It gives the reader permission to think grander, dream bigger, and deliver on that promise by providing activities and frameworks that make the hard work of growth and success a great deal easier. Dr. Holloway offers a fresh and practical approach to follow for leaders who want to harness their drive to win."

- **Dr. Christopher D. Lee, Ph.D., SPHR**, Retired U.S. Marine Corps Lieutenant Colonel; Author of *Performance Conversations: How To Use Questions to Coach Employees, Improve Productivity, and Boost Confidence (Without Appraisals)*

"Life is about how you respond when things get tough. *Win By 100* is more than a leadership book. It is a reminder that with the right mindset and a clear plan, you can push through challenges and come out stronger. TJ's MADE framework is a solid guide for anyone ready to step up and make the most of every opportunity."

- **Travis Mills**, Retired U.S. Army Staff Sergeant; Founder, Travis Mills Foundation; New York Times Bestselling Author

"As a retired military officer, I've learned that leadership is not about being perfect—it's about making consistent progress under pressure, guided by clarity and conviction. *Win By 100* captures that truth with uncommon precision, offering a framework rooted in wisdom and arming leaders with the tools to grow, adapt, and lead with purpose."

- **Todd Schultz,** Retired U.S. Army Lieutenant Colonel; Former West Point Instructor; Recipient of the Distinguished Flying Cross and Three Bronze Stars

"*Win By 100* avoids the trap of telling people how to lead without providing them tools and showing what that looks like in practice. The M.A.D.E. framework, paired with TJ's real-world experiences, offers clarity for anyone trying to lead themselves or others more effectively."

- **Patrick Veroneau**, CEO, Emery Leadership Group, Author, and Podcast host

"I have personally known T.J. and can attest to the profound influence he has in shaping authentic leadership. *Win By 100* offers a compelling framework that emphasizes character, accountability, and emotional intelligence—truly a valuable addition to any leader's journey."

- **Dr. Matthew Ward**, President and CEO, Faith Bible College International

Win By 100

T. J. Holloway

The Holloway Group
19 Elliott Circle
Glenburn, ME 04401

https://themadeleader.com/

Printed in the United States of America by BookBaby

Paperback First Edition

ISBN: 979-8-9943438-3-8

Price: $15.99

Layout and typesetting by Yellow Barn Literary

Dedication

This book is dedicated to my parents, Dr. Johnny and Deborah Holloway.

Thank you for the sacrifices I couldn't see until later in life, and the lessons I had to learn—whether I was ready or not.

Thank you for giving me permission to be fully myself, and for teaching me to honor God in all I do.

I hope I've made you proud.

Contents

Foreword

By Bob Montgomery-Rice, CEO, Bangor Savings Bank, Northern New England's Largest Mutual Bank

In a world where power is often mistaken for leadership and victory is sometimes pursued at the expense of ethics, this book offers a refreshing and necessary truth: the greatest leaders win not by sacrificing others, but by uplifting them. Leadership, in its truest form, is not a performance; it is a promise. A promise to act with integrity, to lead with respect, and to make decisions that reflect care for the people who count on us: our employees, our customers, and our communities.

TJ Holloway has written more than a guide—he's created a blueprint for building organizations that thrive by putting people first. As someone who's had the privilege of sharing a leadership journey with TJ while serving as CEO of Northern New England's largest mutual bank, I can attest that the principles laid out in these pages aren't just thoughtful—they're lived. We've led through challenges and triumphs alike, always grounded in a shared belief that great leadership is defined by service, authenticity, and trust.

This book doesn't tell you how to climb the ladder by stepping on someone else's shoulders. Instead, it shows how to build a foundation so rooted in values that everyone rises together. TJ challenges the conventional wisdom that results are the only metric of success and redefines winning as the ability to meet your goals without compromising your principles.

Here, leadership is not about charisma alone or clever strategy. It's about character. It's about making choices that align with a moral compass, even when no one is watching. It's about fostering workplaces where employees are empowered and seen as vital contributors, not cogs in a machine. It's about designing customer experiences that are not just profitable, but thoughtful, humane, and enduring. And above all, it's about recognizing that the true impact of any organization is not measured in spreadsheets, but in lives changed and communities strengthened.

Whether you're leading a small team or a global enterprise, TJ Holloway's insights will help you balance the pursuit of excellence with the stewardship of values. You'll find tools for building trust, cultivating empathy, and navigating complexity with clarity and purpose. And you'll be reminded that success with integrity isn't just possible, it's transformational.

If you believe leadership can be noble, and that respect is a strength—not a weakness—then this book will speak directly to you.

May it inspire you to lead boldly, win honorably, and make a difference that lasts.

Introduction

It's Winning Time!

I didn't always think this way.

There was a time when I was careful about how I talked about winning—like if I said it out loud, I might offend someone or look arrogant. I'd wrap my goals in softer words, so they sounded more palatable.

"I just want to do well."

"I just want to improve."

I quietly felt like a liar. Because that wasn't the whole story. I wanted to win.

And so do you.

You might hide it. You might dress it up. But deep down, you want to come out on top—in your work, in your relationships, in life.

Somewhere along the way, the world convinced us that wanting to win was something to be ashamed of. Somehow it became more noble to aim for "good enough" than to go for the best. But here's the thing: the people who change the world, in any industry or arena, never apologize for wanting to win. And they win. Consistently.

Be honest—when's the last time you felt like it was okay to say you wanted to win out loud?

Not "show up."

Not "do your best."

Not "make memories."

I mean win.

I bet it's been a while. And that's exactly what I hope to change in these pages.

This past fall, nearly every weekend I was at my son Jaxon's Saturday soccer games—second-grade community rec league. You know the kind: neon jerseys, juice boxes at halftime, parents and sibs on the sidelines, either shivering or sweating in their folding camp chairs.

Here's the kicker (soccer pun intended)—they *don't keep score*. Not officially. It drove Jaxon absolutely bonkers. If I'm honest, it drove me a little nuts, too.

You can look at the two of us and tell that Jax is my *mini-me*. But he doesn't just look like me—he's got my fire, my focus, my drive. And while the coaches encouraged fun and fairness, he couldn't ignore the one thing every true competitor wants to know:

"Did I win?"

I'd tell him, "Focus on the game," biting my tongue so I didn't openly dismiss all the feel-good fluff being taught. But after each game, the second we got in the truck—before I could even press the ignition—he'd turn to me (his covert scorekeeper), eyes small and locked in, and ask:

"Who won, Dad? Who won?"

Not a suggestion. Not a casual ask.

A demand. A need.

Even at seven years old, he had to know where he stood. Did he come out on top? Did his effort mean something and produce the desired result?

You've heard the line a thousand times: "It's not whether you win *or* lose—it's how you play the game."

It's cute.

But it's also not true.

That's what people say when they're trying to make losing feel better. It's comfort talk. It's what you say to your kid when they finish twelfth in the spelling bee, but you still want to hit Dairy Queen.

But let's be real. You came to *win*. To grow. To lead. To build something that matters. And you shouldn't have to apologize for that.

We all have that fire I see in Jaxon at seven. But somewhere along the way, the world tells us to temper it. We're taught that wanting to win is selfish. That ambition is arrogant. That excellence makes other people uncomfortable. So we play it small, hide behind "good enough," and wonder why we feel stuck.

Let me be very real with you.

This idea that everybody's a winner is crap.

The only thing that makes you a winner . . . is *winning*.

If *everyone* gets a trophy, then *no one* is a champion.

So, how the heck are we supposed to *become* winners when we're too scared to even *say* we want to win?

One of my favorite exercises in every leadership seminar I facilitate is to have people write down their biggest fear, anonymously. Then I read them out loud. A person's age, title, or industry doesn't matter. I always see the same thing: *fear of failure*.

"I'm afraid of failing."

"I'm afraid of letting down the people who count on me."

"I'm afraid of not being enough."

Every now and then, someone throws in something random like "grasshoppers" or some freak disease.

But 95 percent of the time? The fear is failure.

Fear of failure is the monster in the room.

And when we break it down, what's failure, really?

It's not winning.

But no life story is a straight line. No person or team leads from start to finish.

Maybe you lose a quarter.

Perhaps you fumble a possession.

Possibly you hit a slump in your relationship.

But you stay in the game.

You don't win by *never losing*. You win by *never quitting*.

That's the difference between being *developed* and being *discouraged.*

And that's where this book begins—with the truth nobody wants to say out loud, but everybody needs to hear:

You're allowed to want to win. In fact, if you're going to lead—if you're going to grow—you'd better start keeping score.

This book is about owning your desire to win. It's about stepping into the raw, real, and messy work of self-leadership—carrying ambition in one hand and respect in the other. If, like Jaxon, you're tired of playing small ball, tired of pretending that just showing up, breaking a sweat, and sharing a few laughs with teammates is enough, and you're ready to pursue the success you deserve, this book is for you.

You want to win.

I want you to win, too.

So let's get after it—*together.*

1

Win By 100

I'll never forget the first time I sat down with Bob Montgomery-Rice (BMR), then the newly declared CEO of Bangor Savings Bank (BSB). At the time, I was teaching undergraduate college courses on corporate topics, but ironically, I'd *never* been face-to-face with a corporate leader.

It all started with a chance encounter while I was teaching in the Business Management Department at Eastern Maine Community College. I met Bob's Chief of Staff, Wendy Durrah, during a community-related project. Wendy and I got along famously. We were collaborating on a board report one day when out of nowhere she said, "Bob would love you."

At that moment, it didn't mean much to me. I had no idea who Bob was. I was so green—soaking wet behind the ears and barely figuring things out. I was thirty-three years young, and pretty good at pretending to know what I was doing. Though deep down, I knew I was out of my depth most of the time. Still, I wanted to *win* in life, and that desire made me willing to endure the discomfort of new and intimidating situations. Wendy set up a meeting for me to meet with BMR the following week.

I was already shaking in my boots just walking into the building. Bob's office, where I was waiting, was pristine. Every second that passed felt heavier than the last. I wasn't sure I was ready for this.

My first thought when the door slid open and BMR walked in?

Dang, this guy is tack sharp.

He looked like he'd stepped straight out of a movie. Pierce Brosnan in *The Thomas Crown Affair* came to mind. His tie alone looked more expensive than my entire outfit. But then movies like *The Untouchables* and *The Godfather* occurred to me, too. I mean, only mob bosses wear cufflinks, *right*?

Everything about him carried that Marlon Brando energy—timeless, composed, like he'd stepped out of a black-and-white film with a quiet kind of power. He even smelled incredible. It definitely wasn't Old Spice. And it wasn't Brut by Fabergé either. I'd never smelled anything like it before, and it made me feel even more out of my league. No, this had to be one of those rare French or Italian fragrances—some *eau de* something I'd never find, couldn't afford, and probably couldn't even pronounce.

BMR didn't say a word as he smoothly brushed by me, circled around his desk, and sat down slow and measured in his dark leather, executive-style chair.

Then, he just looked at me.

Not a casual glance but a Wild West cowboy-to-cowboy kind of stare-down.

I kid you not—it was a full-on, locked-in, at least ten-second gaze that felt like an eternity. My nerves were firing on all cylinders. My palms were lakes. My brain was scrambling for what to say, but the silence just stretched on.

He was clearly in control. And finally, he broke the silence—but not like a normal person would. He didn't say "good morning" or ask if I "found the place okay." Instead, after all those seconds of silence and scrutiny, he looked straight at me and said:

"I like to win."

Just like that. No cap. No exaggeration.

Literally, those are the *exact* first words BMR *ever* said to me.

At this point, BMR was yet to crack a smile. Smiling is the first thing a normal person does when they meet someone new. But I was quickly learning that BMR was *not* normal.

I like to win. Right out of the gate. *How was I supposed to respond to that?* I was frozen. My head a little light, armpits a little greasy.

Honestly, I felt a flicker of anger rise in that moment. *Is this guy trying to punk me?* I thought. Still, somehow, I managed to stammer a response.

"Yes, *sir*. I like to win, too."

I cracked a slight, nervous smile after my response. But BMR didn't relent. Further intensifying what was already the most extreme moment of my young corporate life, he leaned forward, eyed me down like he could see straight through me.

"No. You don't understand." His voice was slightly more concentrated, his eyes in an incredibly lean squint. "I like to win *by a 100 . . .* "

I didn't know what to do. I was scrambling for something to say, but nothing came. More seconds ticked by, and he could see I had nothing. Absolutely nothing.

And that's when BMR threw me a lifeline. His eyes and tone softened.

He said, "But I have to do it while treating *everybody* with dignity and respect."

With that one absolutely beautiful line, I knew I was *all in* for whatever his plan was to be.

That line didn't just change the conversation; *it changed me*. It wasn't just *what* BMR

said; it was the clarity with which he said it. Winning wasn't just a desire for him—it was a *declaration.* He owned it unapologetically. And that last piece, about *dignity and respect*, hit me like a lightning bolt. It was everything I believed but had never been able to put into words. Winning wasn't wrong. But how you win? Yeah, that definitely matters.

In the very next breath, BMR showed me what that looked like.

He finally leaned back in his chair, and for the first time, a smile broke across his face—measured, warm, and real. It wasn't for show. It was the kind of smile that feels like a hand on your back, letting you know you're safe. The air changed. He chuckled lightly and started asking about me—not my résumé, but *me*. My story. My mission. My *why*. The tension melted, and the exchange became human.

It was in that moment that I realized something: he *had planned this entire arc*. The intensity wasn't just a vibe—it was a tool. He wielded it with surgical precision, letting it press just long enough to test my resolve . . . and then releasing me with a grace that told me I *belonged.* He knew exactly when to push, when to pause, and when to pour warmth back into the room. He *delivered* me right into a moment of self-belief.

That's when I saw the truth: I wasn't just dealing with a successful executive. I was sitting in front of an emotional genius. A man who knew how to shape moments that stick with people. A leader who didn't just talk about dignity but demonstrated it. The kind of leader who knows that intensity sets the tone, but authenticity seals the connection.

Say It Out Loud

That day in his office, BMR taught me that winning in life wasn't just about grinding harder than everyone else or playing by the rules.

The truth is hard work doesn't always pay off—not right away—and sometimes not at all. And, yeah, sadly cheaters do win sometimes.

But the people who *really* win—the ones who walk away with peace, pride, and power—are the ones who have the courage to say out loud: "I want to win."

They're the ones who own that ambition unapologetically, who chase it down with

discipline, and who do it without compromising their integrity. That's what separates contenders from pretenders. Not the hustle. Not the highlight reel. But the guts to declare your intent and the character to chase it the right way.

That's what BMR does. And that's why he's *not normal* (in all the *right ways*).

And that's exactly what this book is here to help you do: *to be less normal.*

Let's be real, most of today's "normal" leadership sucks. It's passive, unclear, insecure, and performative. It checks boxes and avoids real accountability. And I have zero interest in being part of that. I'm guessing you don't either.

So I wrote this book to help you unlearn everything about leadership that's average, hollow, or just plain ineffective. To help you lose what's normal, replacing it with what's real, strong, and actually works.

Everything I'm writing here came to me one quiet afternoon while sitting in Mike Howell's chair. Mike's the best barber in the game. I was getting a beard trim, watching silver hairs fall like snow against the black apron wrapped around my neck.

Each one was a sharp, little reminder: I wasn't some fresh-out-the-box rookie anymore. I've stood in corporate war rooms with execs and sat shoulder to shoulder in the trenches with team leads, project managers, and new leaders trying to find their footing. I've earned every one of those grays by walking the path with people willing to do the work of real growth.

And in that moment, as the clippers hummed and I sat still, I felt one thing above all else: *gratitude*. Grateful to have witnessed so many people reclaim their agency. Grateful for the trust they placed in me. Grateful to be part of their journey—not above it, but beside them.

Because when someone invites you into their growth, it's not a small thing. It's sacred work. And it comes with a responsibility—not just to help them succeed, but to help them do it the *right* way.

That's why this book isn't about hollow wins.

It's about leading without losing yourself.

It's about staying grounded while leveling up.

It's about building something you don't have to apologize for later.

If success costs you your integrity, then it's not success—it's just a more expensive failure.

The ABCD Model: A Winning Cycle

When you strip away all the noise, winning in life boils down to understanding and consistently executing a simple, repeatable process—a winning cycle I call my ABCD Model.

Whether you're building a career, launching a product, or trying to make your mark, the ABCD Model is a universal roadmap for moving forward in life and finding success.

Here's how it works.

A is for Attention: The First Domino

The first step to getting anywhere in life is capturing people's attention. Without attention, nothing else matters. You could have the best product, the most innovative idea, or the talent of a lifetime, but if no one notices, it's all for nothing. Attention is the gateway—everything starts here.

I've heard people boldly proclaim, "I don't care what other people think about me," wearing it like a badge of honor. Let me be blunt: *that's dumb.*

How can you *not care* what people think about you? The way others perceive you is the only reason you've ever found any level of success in your life. Their perception—fair or not—determines whether doors will open for you or stay shut. To not care what others think of you is to not care about your own achievement.

Think of attention like sunlight and talent as a solar panel. If the panel's in the shade, no light equals no energy. Same with you. No visibility equals no impact.

Be real—what about you stops people mid-scroll? What makes people put down their pens, lean toward you, and really pay attention to what you're saying? What do they remember after you leave the room? What earns you that second look?

Attention is the first domino—once you tip it, the rest of the cycle begins.

B is for Belief

Once you've got someone's attention, here's the part too many people sleep on:

You better shape the belief they form about you—fast. Because not all attention is good attention.

If they notice you, but they decide you're sloppy, unreliable, or full of bull? You're done. They'll smile in the meeting and blacklist you in the hallway. *Worse?* Some won't just ignore you—they'll actively get in your way.

A negative belief spreads faster than the truth, and once it sticks, good luck unsticking it.

But when someone believes in you—really believes? Now you've got traction. Now doors start to open. Because belief is the bridge between attention and opportunity. And without that bridge? Your moment fizzles. Your momentum dies.

Here's what people forget: It doesn't matter how smart, talented, or hardworking you are.

If the people above you don't believe in you, you're not getting the next shot. Belief moves power. It moves trust. It moves careers. And it doesn't just flow up the ladder—it trickles down, too.

If your team doesn't believe in you, they won't run through walls for you. They won't stay late. They won't back your calls. They'll nod in the meetings and check out the second you walk away. Belief is the currency. Not talent. Not charm. Not even results. Because none of those get you anywhere if nobody's willing to bet on you.

So ask yourself: *What do people believe when they see you?* Not what do you *hope* they believe—*what's the real story you're telling, just by how you show up?* Because belief builds trust. And then trust builds everything else.

In late 2019, I was consulting for the CEO of a midsize sign company in New England. It was a family business—recently handed down from father to son—and the transition had been rough. The father earned loyalty through relationships and respect. But the son? Command-and-control all day. People noticed. Revenue slipped. Key talent left. The leadership team was scrambling.

That's when I got called in. The CEO said, "Fix my leadership team." That phrase always raises a red flag to me. Because leadership problems almost always start at the top. And I had a hunch this was no exception.

After a few interviews and assessments, it was clear—the team wasn't failing due to incompetence. They were failing because the CEO had created a culture where people didn't feel seen, valued, or respected.

Despite his curt demeanor, I wanted to help. I especially wanted to help his direct reports—the ones enduring his underdeveloped leadership forty-plus hours a week. And I knew step one would be to assist him in gaining *self-awareness*. He needed to see that some of the breakdown was on him. So I recommended the tool I trust most: the Leadership Effectiveness Analysis 360. I've used it hundreds of times to help leaders get honest, bias-protected feedback on how they're actually perceived.

I laid it out: "If you don't know how your people *experience you and your leadership*, how can you lead them? Their perception of you shapes your effectiveness, your influence, and this company's future."

I was proud of my pitch—clear, objective, respectfully delivered.

He barely looked up.

"Experience me and my leadership?" he scoffed. "I don't care how they experience me. Last I checked, it's my name on the sign out front."

I paused.

That wasn't just arrogance—it was recklessness, the kind that comes from power inherited, not earned. He was staring at his name on the sign like it proved he was a leader. Meanwhile, I was staring at the cracks in the culture—the writing on the wall he refused to read.

I'd pegged him already. Bold. Smug. Liked to swing first. So I met him on his turf.

"Well," I said, "that's dumb."

His head snapped up.

"Come again?"

"That's stupid," I said calmly. My own BMR glare locked in. Zero flinch.

"Your name is on the sign," I said, "but every paycheck your people take home, every sale this place closes, every ounce of momentum you've got? That came from your dad. He built this. Not you. And now it's your turn to *earn* what he left you."

I leaned in and continued.

"If you don't care how your people experience you, you *are* the problem. At least a part of it. And if you keep leading like that? This place is going to collapse under the weight of your ego."

Silence. Not the awkward kind—the suffocating kind. Then, right on cue, his wife walked in. Arms full of mail. Two coffees in hand. She paused mid-step—like she'd just walked into a house on fire.

I nodded in her direction. Tight smile. She nodded back, eyes darting between us, picking up the heat, realizing quickly that one of those coffees would not be needed.

Then he leaned in, voice low and sharp, "You can leave now."

No wince. I gave him a nod. Tighter smile.

"Yes," I said. "Gladly."

I flung my jacket over my shoulder like a cape. Because in that moment it was a cape. I wasn't just a fixer walking out of that building—I was a titan. A force. A superhero stepping out for every employee who's ever suffered under a big title-holder who never took the time to learn how to lead.

That was the first time I'd been pissed off at a client. Wouldn't be the last. But I knew the truth: The problem wasn't his people. It was him. *His ego. His blind spots.* His refusal to lead from within.

He thought "strong leadership" meant never caring what others think. But that wasn't strength—it was fragility in disguise. Caring what people think of you isn't weakness—it's wisdom. Their belief in you shapes everything: their trust, their buy-in, their willingness to go to battle with you. If you ignore that? You might still have the title. But you've already lost the team.

This CEO failed to care about how his people saw him. And that failure became a brand that calcified into his reputation. And that deserved reputation triggered the fall of a family business built on the back of his father. I hated to see it go out that way. But the revolving door started spinning. Talent walked. Trust eroded. Culture cracked. And like that? Down goes Frazier!

The headlines blamed the company's shutdown on COVID-19. But I know the truth. One man's ego had been infecting that culture long before the pandemic.

The place didn't die from a public health crisis. It died from a leadership crisis.

So, I ask again, what beliefs have others formed about you?

Not what you *say* you stand for.

Not what your *title* implies.

Not what you *wish* they saw.

What do they *actually* believe?

Whether you like it or not, you don't control the narrative in other people's heads. But you control *what you model*. You control *what you tolerate*. You control *how you show up*.

Your reputation isn't what you say in the meeting. It's what people whisper after you leave.

C is for Chance

If someone has paid attention to you and formed a positive belief in you, that same someone is likely to give you a chance. And chances? Chances are everything.

If belief is the bridge, a chance is the open door. A signal that someone believes in you enough to risk a little on your behalf. It's your shot to prove what you're made of, to show what you can do, to earn your way forward.

Here's something most people miss. The people who win the most? They're not always the most talented. They're the ones who get the most chances. Because the more chances you get, the more likely you are to win. It's just math.

You're not guaranteed success, but you are guaranteed growth. With every opportunity—win or lose—your experience sharpens, your aim improves, your confidence builds. And yeah, sometimes the second shot is the one that changes everything.

Back in junior high, I lived for Friday pep rallies. The noise. The energy. The chaos. It lit something up in me. One particular pep day, the gym was electric—bleachers packed, PA system thumping, students cheering like it was Game 7. Then the emcee—one of our assistant principals—grabbed the mic and fired up the crowd:

"All right, folks! One lucky student is going to shoot their best shot for twenty-five smackeroos! But not just any shot—a three-pointer from the top of the key!"

Now, this was right around the time the three-point line had been introduced in North Carolina schools. It was fresh, it was buzzworthy—and I guess they wanted to have some fun with it.

And twenty-five dollars? That made you a *middle-school millionaire!* Enough to buy snacks for the week *and* treat your buddies like royalty.

The emcee reached into the box of names, drew a slip, and called out . . . "TJ Holloway."

I bounced down those bleachers fast—like Bob Barker had just called me on *The Price is Right*. Heart pounding. Palms sweaty. Every eye in the gym locked on me. I grabbed the ball and jogged to the top of the key (while trying to look cool).

Now, I was the starting shooting guard for the Neal Middle School Eagles. I *knew* this gym. I *knew* this shot. *But this time?* It felt like I was shooting to save the world. I lined it up. Took a deep breath in. Focused hard on the center of the rim. Exhaled, and let it rip.

BOINK!

Back rimmed it. Just a little too much juice.

The crowd let out a collective groan. I was just glad I didn't shoot an airball in front of all those kids—my teammates would've never let me live that down. I shook my head, grinning, and turned to walk back to my seat in the stands. But then—something unexpected happened. That assistant principal picked up the ball, looked at me, and smiled.

"Let's give him one more chance," he said into the mic.

The gym went nuts. And here's why that moment still hits me to this day: That same assistant principal had seen me earlier that week out by the cafeteria's stubborn side door, holding it open for one of our classmates in a wheelchair. I propped the door open with my back. Made sure their wheels didn't catch on the frame. Waited until they were all the way through before I moved on. The assistant principal was the only one watching, and he gave me one of those small nods—the kind that says, "I see who you really are."

When I missed that shot, he didn't just see a miss—he saw a kid who showed up when no one was watching. He saw someone worth rooting for. And *I think* that's why he gave me another chance.

I grabbed the ball. Squared up, trusted the muscle memory, and let it fly.

Another *BOINK*.

But this one hit dead center on the backboard square, bounced straight in, and was followed by the sound of redemption. *SWISHHH!!!*

The gym exploded. Kids jumped up. High-fives everywhere. The bank was open—and it put bank in my pocket. I was grinning so wide my face hurt. That second chance didn't just earn me twenty-five bucks (which I immediately blew on Bojangles chicken and biscuits for some of my teammates). It taught me that the miss wasn't the end of the story—it was just part of the setup.

Chances aren't charity. They're earned. Through consistency. Through character. Through fostering a belief in you by others. How you treat people when no one's clapping. How you handle disappointment without quitting.

That CEO I told you about earlier? He wasn't losing just sales—he was losing chances. Because his people didn't believe in him anymore. And when belief breaks, chances stop showing up.

On the flip side, I've worked with rising leaders who weren't the flashiest or loudest. But they kept earning chance after chance. Why? Because they were solid. Respectful. Accountable. They showed up for their people, and their people showed up for them.

So let me ask you—straight up: Would you give yourself a chance?

If the answer is "maybe," good. That means there's still room to grow. And this book?

This book is your next shot. Not your last. Not your only. Just the next.

D is for Deliver

A chance (even a second chance) means nothing if you don't deliver.

You can have all the *attention* in the world. You can earn *belief.* You can be handed the golden opportunity (your *chance*). But if you fumble it—if you ghost when it gets real, if you show up small when you were given the stage—your chance becomes a waste.

Attention, belief, and chance all rely to some degree on other people. But delivery? *That's all on you.*

To deliver means you show up when it matters. Not when it's easy. Not when it's convenient. When it counts. It means you don't disappear under pressure. You don't wait for perfect conditions. You don't make excuses, dodge responsibility, or coast on talent. You execute. Period.

Because delivering isn't about being flashy. It's about being consistent. And when you do that—when you stack wins, when you follow through, when you become the one people can count on? Something shifts. You stop chasing attention—because now, you command it.

Early in the cycle, attention is something you chase. You raise your hand. You speak up. You put yourself out there. But if you keep delivering—over time, or in one undeniable moment—everything changes. You stop chasing attention . . . *because it starts chasing you.*

My wife and I had just come back from a trip where we grabbed a fresh pineapple. Once home, I set it in the fruit bowl on the kitchen island with the apples and oranges. Our son Jace was about a year and a half old, and it occurred to me by the way he stared at it that he'd never seen a pineapple before.

You should've seen him when he first spotted it—looking at it like it was a threat to national security. Spiky, weird, uninviting. Every time he walked by, he leaned away with full-on skepticism. The kid wanted no part of it.

A few days later, my wife sliced it up—cubed it nice, laid it out on a plate like little golden gems. The spikes were gone, and the yellow, juicy flesh glistened under the kitchen lights. It looked way more appetizing—like something out of a Del Monte ad.

We offered Jace a bite, knowing he'd love it. But that boy panicked. Hot tears, head whipping side to side, arms flailing like I was trying to poison him. I'm not exaggerating—I had to *hold this child down like he was getting a tetanus shot*. Full dad mode. I'm talking borderline full nelson just to rub a slice of pineapple on his lips.

But then—*boom!*

His eyes got big. His mouth stopped fighting. His whole face changed. It was like a switch flipped: *"Wait . . . this junk is delicious."*

Next thing I know, he's eating pineapple like it's going out of style. Couldn't get enough.

To this day, he chases pineapple. Wants the fruit cups in his lunchbox. Reminds his mom to grab the fresh, pre-cut chunks from the deli. Pineapple used to be a once-in-a-while thing in our house—now it's a staple, all because one day, it delivered.

That's what happens when something (or someone) delivers.

People fight. Reject. Avoid. But when the real thing hits, it changes everything.

When your work delivers, people remember.

They lean in. They come back. They tell other people.

So, what are you doing with the chances you've already been given?

Not the ones you're hoping for. Not the ones you think you deserve.

The ones already in the fruit bowl—right now.

Are you delivering?

Because, let's be honest, some chances show up looking spiky, weird, and uninviting.

Sometimes we dodge what could actually help us grow.

But once you deliver—and once people get a taste—everything changes.

The Cycle of Success

Think of the ABCD Model as a flywheel, not a checklist. It's a repeatable force that builds on itself, gaining momentum and power, helping you cement habits that lead to consistently winning by 100.

Attention earns you the glance.

Belief earns you their trust.

Chance gives you the shot.

Delivery seals the deal.

Once you deliver, the wheel starts spinning again. Only now—it spins faster. Stronger. Harder. You're not just noticed. You're known.

This cycle isn't optional. It's happening around you and to you whether you realize it or not. Life doesn't care about your potential—it reflects your patterns. If you say you're delivering but your results don't match, life will call your bluff. Not with a warning—but with silence. Missed calls. Ghosted emails. Opportunities that don't knock twice. Life doesn't lie. It holds up a mirror and lets your momentum—or lack of it—speak for itself.

Every leader you admire. Every artist you love. Every underdog who made it. They didn't just stumble into greatness. They mastered this cycle. They fought for attention, earned belief, seized their shot, and when the moment came, they showed up and delivered.

That's how reputations are built, legacies are born, and people go from under-the-radar to undeniable.

So, where are *you* in the cycle?

Are you still fighting to be seen? Trying to rebuild belief? Waiting on a shot that hasn't come? Or are you standing at the edge of delivery, needing to prove what you're made of?

Wherever you are—own it. Name it. Then move with intention. Because here's the bottom line: You don't rise to the level of your dreams. You rise to the level of your consistency.

This model doesn't just get you in the game. It teaches you how to win by 100. Just like BMR.

Every.

Single.

Time.

2

MADE

You know that feeling? The one where you're doing everything “right” but still feel stuck—like you're running in place and trapped?

Maybe you're a manager watching your team spin its wheels. You’ve got solid people. The skills are there. But the spark is missing. Or maybe it’s just you, staring at your own reflection, thinking, *I know I’m capable of more—so why does it feel like I’m stuck in neutral? Why doesn’t my boss recognize my potential?*

Let’s acknowledge that your desire to win *is there.* Your hunger *is real.* But something just isn’t clicking. And if you’re tired of waiting for a breakthrough that never comes, it’s time to shift gears and figure out what’s holding you back.

You’re not the problem*!*

Your team’s *probably* not the problem either*!*

The real issue is the system we’ve all been trained to trust. The books. The workshops. The online courses. The slick certification programs crooning their ads on LinkedIn. The ones that promise to change everything—but nothing actually changes. They check every box, but they still leave us stuck. *Why?*

Because we are drowning in *training* and thirsting for *development.*

Training tells us *what to do*. Development transforms how we *think,* how we *lead,* how we *show up.* Training *checks boxes*. Development builds *character*. Training makes you *competent*. Development makes you *impactful.*

The MADE System: A Blueprint for Creating Developed Leadership

Great leaders don't happen by accident. They're not born. They're *built.* They're *made.*

This chapter introduces MADE—Motivation, Assessment, Declaration, Execution—a simple system for turning competence into real, developed leadership that can help you win by 100.

Too many people walk around with titles they haven't earned. My dad used to say: "Everybody gets older, but not everyone grows up." And he was right. Most leaders never get there. They stop growing. They settle for "good enough." They confuse managing tasks with leading people.

Underdeveloped leadership isn't just a personal issue—it's a silent anchor that drags down teams, stifles innovation, and kills culture from the inside out. You see it in missed goals. In the exhaustion people can't name. In the turnover nobody wants to talk about.

The signs are everywhere:

- Leaders who fold when the heat rises because they've never built resilience
- Managers who hit numbers but can't hold trust
- Teams who know how to do the work but don't know how to work together

And people—good people—crippled by imposter syndrome, because no one ever developed them past technical skill.

The good news: once you can see it, you can start to fix it. And that's where growth begins—not with another training, but with a brutally honest question:

"How much of this is because of me?"

Good leadership is crucial to winning. And good leadership doesn't start with org charts or buzzwords. It starts in the mirror. The cracks you ignore in yourself always show up in your team.

Just as ABCD is the cycle that will keep you moving toward wins, the MADE System is your blueprint for closing those leadership gaps to ensure that cycle realizes its true potential.

In the pages ahead, through a combination of stories and activities, we'll name the chief culprits I've most often seen holding back leaders and teams (the seven gaps), give you a quick-reset tool you can use today (the "Other AAA"), and then show how MADE turns those insights into durable change.

Mind Your Gaps

When leadership starts to slip, it rarely happens all at once. It's small—an unchecked habit here, a missed conversation there. You don't notice the foundation shifting until something finally cracks. After years of coaching and leading teams, I've learned to spot the early warning signs. These seven cracks show up almost everywhere—and if you can name them, you can fix them.

1. Accountability Isn't Happening—You've Let Standards Slip

You don't have an accountability problem—you have a leadership problem.

Someone misses a deadline, and you think, *"It's not worth the fight."* You tell yourself you'll handle it later. But *later* never comes. A week goes by, and suddenly, that standard you thought was non-negotiable . . . it's negotiable now.

The truth is that when you let things slide, you're not being kind. You're being careless. Your team is watching you, and every time you brush off an excuse or let a deadline slip, you're silently teaching them that results don't really matter. Effort? *Optional.* Standards? *Flexible.*

So, ask yourself:

- When was the last time you held someone accountable and followed through?
- Are you sending a message that "close enough" is good enough?

Accountability isn't about catching people doing wrong—it's about setting them up to do *right.* It's about making sure everyone knows the bar, believes in the bar, and feels the weight of letting it drop.

Here's your challenge: Think about the last missed deadline or unmet expectation of your team. Did you let it slide? If you did, name it. Own it. Then do something about it—today. Because accountability isn't a dirty word. It's the foundation of every high-performing team.

2. Communication Breakdowns—Mixed Signals All Day Long

Your team isn't failing because they're confused—they're failing because you are.

When you're not clear, your team starts guessing. And guesswork doesn't just waste time—it burns people out. It frustrates them, discourages them, and leaves them feeling like they're playing a game they don't understand. Straight up, that's on you.

Here's your gut check:

- Are people constantly asking for clarification because they don't get it?
- Do you find yourself re-explaining tasks or cleaning up work that missed the mark?

Clarity isn't optional—it's your job. A team can't perform when they're unsure about the goal, the plan, or their role in it. Communication isn't about sounding smart—it's about making sure everyone knows *exactly* what needs to happen and why.

Here's your challenge: Take a moment today and look at your last few emails or instructions. Were they crystal clear? If not, rewrite them. Be specific. Be direct. Stop leaving people to guess—and start leading them to succeed.

3. Developing Your People Is Not on Your Radar

If you're not growing your team, you're managing tasks—not leading people.

You've got a great team. They're good at their jobs. But here's the problem: "good" isn't good enough if they're not growing. Development isn't about getting today's work done—it's about preparing people for what's next. And if you're not actively lifting your team *up*, you're holding them *down*.

Ask yourself:

- Are you giving real feedback, or are you just checking the box?

- Are you challenging people to stretch, or are they stuck in the same patterns?

The best leaders don't just manage—they build. They help people uncover potential they didn't even know they had. If your team isn't growing, it's not just their failure—it's yours, too.

Here's your challenge: Identify one person on your team who could do more with the right push. Set up a conversation. Give them real feedback. Challenge them to step up—and then support them as they do.

4. Low Morale and Disengagement—The Energy Is Flat

Your team isn't lazy—they're starving for recognition.

Here's a hard truth: people don't come to work to punch a clock. They want to feel valued, respected, and *seen.* If your team's energy feels flat, it's not because they don't care—it's because they don't think *you* do.

Ask yourself:

- When was the last time you genuinely recognized someone's hard work?
- Are people giving you their best, or just the bare minimum to get by?

Recognition doesn't cost you a thing, but disengagement? That'll cost you *everything*—performance, retention, and trust. People need to know what they do matters.

Here's your challenge: Tomorrow, call out someone's hard work—not with a generic "good job," but with specific, meaningful praise. Watch how quickly recognition turns "bare minimum" into "above and beyond."

5. Organizational Values Aren't Real—They're Just Words on a Wall

If you're not living your values, they're meaningless—and everyone knows it.

Here's the deal: values are non-negotiable. They're not fancy posters, company speeches, or catchy slogans. They're the behaviors you model every day. And if your team doesn't see you walking the talk, they'll stop believing in the words altogether.

Ask yourself:

Are you making decisions that align with the values you preach?

Would your team say you live those values, even when no one's watching?

Integrity doesn't happen in *meetings*—it happens in *moments*. Leadership starts with consistency, and values only mean something when you prove they're real.

Here's your challenge: Write down the values you claim to stand for. Now, ask yourself: "Do my actions prove these values, or am I just talking a good game?"

6. Conflict Avoidance—Hoping Problems Will Solve Themselves

Conflict avoided is conflict multiplied. Period.

My favorite CEO (we'll talk about him later) often says, "Problems don't age well." He's right. And here's what happens when you dodge hard conversations: small frustrations grow into resentment. Resentment grows into dysfunction. And dysfunction destroys teams. Problems don't solve themselves—they get worse.

So, ask yourself:

- Are you avoiding a tough talk because it feels uncomfortable?
- Do you cross your fingers and hope the issue will just disappear?

It won't. Leaders face conflict head-on—not because they like it, but because it's their job. You have to do your job . . . especially the parts you don't like.

Here's your challenge: Think about the hard conversation you've been avoiding. Write down what you need to say. Then, go have the talk—this week.

7. Guiding Principles Are Confusing Everyone

When you confuse values and principles, you create chaos.

Values are your foundation—they're the non-negotiables. Principles? They're flexible—they guide you when the path isn't clear. Underdeveloped leaders mix the two, and when they do, teams lose confidence.

Ask yourself:

- Do you know the difference between your core values and your guiding principles?
- Are you sending a clear message about what's flexible and what's not?

Neither you nor your team can operate in confusion. People need to know where the lines are drawn and where they're allowed to adapt.

Here's your challenge: Clarify the difference today. Write down your values and your principles. Distinguish them. Make them clear, then communicate them to your team and whoever else needs to know.

Make no mistake, at the core of every struggling team is not a lack of talent—it's a lack of leadership. If you're not holding people accountable, communicating with clarity, developing your team, recognizing effort, living your values, addressing conflict, and setting clear principles, then you're not leading—you're managing dysfunction. And dysfunction doesn't fix itself. Leadership is about stepping up, facing the hard truths, and making intentional choices that create strong, engaged, high-performing teams.

So here's the bottom line: If you see yourself in any of these challenges, do something about it. Because leadership isn't about what you say—it's about what you do.

Jumpstart Your Journey to Better Leadership (The Other AAA)

There's nothing like planning a trip to remind you just how chaotic life can be. For years, every vacation or business trip I took felt like an uphill battle: endless hours comparing flights, booking hotels, and juggling schedules. Honestly, it felt like planning some trips took longer than the trips themselves!

One day, I found myself trapped in that same cycle while preparing to travel for a seminar I was to lead in New Jersey. I'd been invited to speak at the Northeast Chapter of the American Association of Airport Executives (NEC/AAAE)—an awesome organization dedicated to developing leaders in the aviation industry. It was an event where the best and brightest emerging leaders in aviation administration gathered annually, and I was booked to deliver a leadership development session.

Everything was falling into place—except the flights.

Hotel? Booked.

Rental car? Handled.

Flights? Not booked. *Not handled.* Just . . . a total hot mess.

I was circling travel sites like a hawk, trying to piece together an itinerary that made sense. Nothing was clicking. No connections aligned. No seats available. No solutions in sight. And then the irony hit me like a punchline from the universe:

I was about to go *help* leaders in the airline industry, but I couldn't even get my own flight situation under control.

Seriously? It felt like the universe was trolling me.

My frustration was rising fast—one of those "if this thing freezes one more time, I swear" moments. Right on cue, my son Jaxon burst through the door, fresh off the school bus, proudly clutching the day's mail . . . and a sticky, half-melted ring from a recently deceased Ring Pop.

He tossed the mail on the counter like it meant nothing.

Turns out—*it meant everything.*

Right there, buried between coupon flyers and grocery store ads, was a promo from AAA Travel Agency. Some vacation-planning thing. But in that moment, I didn't see a beach. I saw *escape*—not from work, but from the mess I'd made trying to plan it.

I picked up the phone, dialed the number, and was connected to someone I can only describe as a travel angel named Brooke.

Brooke didn't just fix my trip. She *rescued* it. No more bouncing between tabs. No more guessing games or frozen screens. No more travel-site-induced migraines.

She listened. She handled it. She *executed* like a boss.

From that day forward, Brooke became my go-to. She doesn't just book my travel—she makes the impossible feel effortless. And when I've got a destination to reach, she's the first call I make.

Just like I needed Brooke to bring clarity and direction to my travel plans, *you* need something to bring clarity and direction to your *leadership journeys.* Because you might have the hotel booked. You might have the rental lined up. But if your internal "flights" aren't clear? If your mindset, your method, and your momentum aren't aligned?

That's where *The Other AAA* comes in.

And no, I'm not talking about the travel club. I'm talking about the three things every leader—every human—needs to move forward with purpose:

Awareness. Acknowledgement. Action.

That's the AAA that gets your leadership off the ground. It's like AAA roadside assistance—but for your leadership, your career, and your life. And trust me—when everything's broken down and the pressure's rising? You don't need cute. You need a tow truck.

The first A stands for Awareness.

Okay. Where are you—*really*?

Where are you in your leadership? In your growth? In your life? Not where your job title says. Not where your Instagram bio suggests. Where are you really?

Are you stuck? Are you spinning your wheels in a role that looks good on paper but feels hollow when you wake up in the morning?

Awareness is about brutal honesty. It's about looking in the mirror and realizing the person holding you back . . . is probably you. You can't grow past what you're afraid to face. You can't fix what you won't name. And you can't get where you want to go if you won't admit where you actually are.

The second A is Acknowledgment.

This is where you stop performing and start owning. No more blaming your boss, your ex, your team, your childhood, your circumstances. You are the common denominator in *every* room you walk into.

That's not a guilt trip—it's a *power move.*

Because if you're the one who drove yourself here, you can also be the one who drives yourself out. Ownership isn't always comfortable, but it's the birthplace of freedom. Like Dr. Phil (McGraw) often says: "You can't change what you don't acknowledge." If you don't claim it, you can't change it. It's that simple.

Now comes the third A: Action!

Awareness without action is just a journal entry. Acknowledgment without action is a motivational speech to yourself. This is where most people stall—waiting for perfect timing, overthinking every move, spinning in preparation mode.

Stop waiting on a sign. You don't need another sign—you need a step.

The perfect moment is a myth—so just take the first step.

Book the flight. Have the conversation. Send the email. Make the ask. Apply for the thing. Say what needs to be said. Do what needs to be done. And if it's messy? *Good!* That means it's real. Awkward progress beats polished procrastination every single time.

Perfection is a trap.

Movement is power.

You don't need to have all the answers before you act. You just need to act. So whatever's been sitting on your heart, your desk, or your to-do list? Handle it. And in the immortal words of Young MC—don't just stand there . . . "bust a move!" Because the life you want? It's not coming to knock. You've got to go get it.

Pack Your Bags and Get Moving

The MADE method works because it's simple, raw, real, and doesn't allow any bull. You don't need a perfect map; you just need to start moving. Where you are today doesn't matter as much as who you're willing to become. Growth demands honesty and effort, but it rewards those who start the journey.

Let's look at two activities that work together. The first helps you get honest about where you are right now and what action you can take today to get unstuck. The second stretches that self-awareness into leadership maturity—showing what "developed" actually looks like in practice and inviting you to grade your own paper.

Activity: Three Truths and an Action!

Take a moment now. Imagine your journey as a leader. *Where do you want to go? What's holding you back?* Below, write down three truths about where you are right now. Then, write one action you can take today to start moving forward.

Truth 1:
Truth 2:
Truth 3:
ACTION!

The real job isn't just to lead—it's to become a fully developed leader. Not just at work, but in your life. This kind of growth doesn't happen overnight. It's not a certificate or a motivational quote. It's a process. A grind. A transformation.

And just like human development moves through distinct stages—from formation, to infancy, to adolescence, and finally adulthood—leadership grows in stages, too. You don't just wake up one day "developed." You grow into it. (Or you don't.)

So what does it actually mean to be *fully developed*?

It means you consistently drive success—not just with results, but with your presence. It means you elevate the room, not just with your ideas, but with your integrity. It means you carry yourself in a way that makes people want to show up better just because you're in the room.

Developed leaders don't have to bark orders to get things done. Their energy alone invites trust, clarity, and alignment. They model resilience, communicate with emotional intelligence, and create teams that actually work.

But let's not sugarcoat it: most people don't get there. *Why?*

Because they stop growing. They settle for *functional* when they should be aiming for *formidable*. They confuse task management with people leadership. And when pressure hits, they fold—not because they're incapable, but because they're *underdeveloped.*

This isn't just a corporate issue. This is a human issue. If you've ever found yourself frustrated by the people around you—by the excuses, the emotional reactions, the breakdown in trust—maybe it's not just them.

Maybe it's you, too.

The chart that follows breaks it down: What developed leaders *actually do*, and what underdeveloped ones don't. Read it slowly. Check yourself. And be honest about where your gaps are. Don't get bitter, get better.

Chart: What a Developed Leader Looks Like

Developed Leaders	What It Looks Like
Follow Basic Instructions	Simple but critical. They respect the process, don't overcomplicate it, and get the basics right every time.
Work & Play as Part of Team	They don't compete—they collaborate. Success is shared, and ego takes a back seat.
Know When to Speak and When to Listen	Timing matters. They don't talk just to hear their own voice. They speak up with purpose and listen with respect, keeping discussions productive.
Are Self-Motivated	Their drive comes from within, not from a deadline or fear of being scolded. They don't need a babysitter.

Handle Conflict Without Retaliation	They stay calm, respond maturely, and focus on solutions—not revenge.
Exercise Social & Emotional Intelligence	They get how their actions impact others and how to respond with emotional maturity.
Embrace a Growth Mindset	They see challenges as opportunities to grow, not threats to avoid.
Seek Feedback & Receive It Well	They ask for feedback to get better and take it humbly, not defensively.
Provide Feedback Respectfully	They give constructive feedback, offer opportunities, and build others up—not tear them down.
Honor Consensus	Once a decision is made, they commit 100 percent—no lingering resentment. They plow forward as if it was their own idea.
Are Assertive, Not Passive-Aggressive	They communicate clearly and respectfully—no doormats, no bullies.

Now, Grade Your Own Paper

Think of this chart as more than a simple list—it's the answer key to life's leadership character quiz. Use it to grade yourself honestly. Yes, *grade your own paper*. That's something MADE leaders do accurately and frequently, and I first learned its power in an unexpected way while working as a professor teaching undergraduate students at Eastern Maine Community College.

While teaching at EMCC, I was also working on my doctoral degree, raising a family, volunteering at my church, and running my consulting business. Time was not a luxury I could afford, so I did everything I could to reclaim a few extra minutes each day.

To streamline the process of grading papers, I had my students grade their own quizzes, some homework assignments, and even some tests. But this approach wasn't just about saving time—it was also an exercise in honesty and accountability.

I'd kick it off with a smirk, saying, "Raise your right hand and repeat after me: I promise . . . to grade my paper accurately. If I don't . . . I owe my professor $100."

They laughed—but they knew I meant business.

Then I'd start going over the answers one by one. And that's when the self-negotiations would kick in:

What if I said something close to that?

Does this phrasing count for partial credit?

Mine's kind of right . . . right?

They weren't just assessing their work—they were actively engaging in the process of evaluating what they'd done well and where they fell short. By the end, they'd write their "soft grade" at the top of the paper, sign their name next to it in honor of the pledge, and hand in the half-scored paper. When I reviewed their work later, the hard part—judging the quality of the answers—was already done. My role became one of verifying their honesty and correcting grades when needed, not starting from scratch, which saved me a good deal of time.

This process worked because it taught a powerful lesson: growth requires self-assessment. And sometimes, we all have to *grade our own papers*. We have to pause, look at the answers we've given in life and be brutally honest about whether they're right, close enough, or completely wrong.

Can you be honest with yourself about where you stand? Where do you excel? Where are you average? Where are you missing the mark altogether?

But here's the catch—just like in my classroom, your self-assessment (how you grade yourself) isn't the final word. Eventually, I'd review my students' work to see if their self-grading was accurate and honest.

Life works the same way. Over time, the truth reveals itself, holding us accountable for the way we've evaluated ourselves. If we've been too lenient, the gaps in our actions will become clear. If we've been too harsh, life may surprise us by highlighting strengths we've overlooked. Either way, life corrects the scores we give ourselves. That's why being honest with your self-assessment is so crucial—it lays the foundation for real growth before life steps in to show you the answers you missed.

Lean Into Your Own Development

The qualities on the Developed Leader *chart* aren't just a checklist—they're a mirror. They reflect the core qualities that make up a well-developed person or leader. Look at these traits carefully and ask yourself: *Which of these do I live out every day? And where do I need to step up?*

Even the best leaders don't check every box perfectly, but here's the difference: they never stop striving. Every one of these traits is learnable. Trainable. Buildable.

When you're a MADE Leader, grading your own paper isn't a one-time thing. It's a lifestyle. Because only when you confront the truth—your strengths, your near misses, your blind spots—can you take steps that actually move you forward.

Where you identify gaps, don't dismiss them or make excuses. Lean into them. Gaps aren't weaknesses—they're growth invitations.

You MADE It!

You made it. This is the moment where things shift. Right here—this is where the MADE System enters the picture. Not as another leadership theory. Not as some feel-good acronym to slap on a slide deck. This is your framework for real, gritty, in-the-trenches growth.

MADE stands for *Motivation, Assessment, Declaration,* and *Execution.* But more than that—it's a looking glass. A challenge. A playbook. A personal call-out.

It doesn't build leaders who rely on their titles, salaries, or the authority stamped on their name badge. It builds leaders whose presence carries weight. People who get things done—because they've done the internal work to earn the external trust.

In the following chapters, we'll look at how each component of the MADE system builds to a whole that gives you the best chance of winning by 100.

There was a time in my life where I looked successful—but I was stuck. I had the degrees. The business cards. The credentials. But behind the scenes? I was surviving more than leading. Performing more than transforming.

I built the MADE system because I needed it. And once I started applying it—honestly, consistently, without ego—it didn't just shift my leadership.

It changed my life.

That's what I want for you. Understand that no one's coming to save your leadership. No mentor, no manager, no keynote speaker can do this for you. I designed MADE to meet you halfway—but you've got to show up. Let's get you MADE.

Starting with M—Motivation.

3

Motivation – (*Mo)*ti(*v)*at(*e)*

A few years back, I was called in to work with Greg—an executive leading the Automation & Digital Services (A&DS) team at a community bank anchored in upstate New York. On paper, Greg's team was loaded with talent—technically sharp, experienced, battle-tested. But behind the scenes, the wheels were coming off.

Efficiency was tanking. Team dynamics were toxic. High performers were brushing off their résumés and eyeing the exits. It was dysfunction on the brink of collapse.

One of the bank's senior leaders—someone I'd worked with years earlier at a top Maine bank—called me. We'd done solid work together before, so the call felt familiar. But the tone was different this time. Urgent. The A&DS team was unraveling. Greg was leading it. And they decided they wanted me to coach him for a full calendar year.

I agreed. And I'll be honest—what I found surprised me.

Greg *wasn't* incompetent. He *wasn't* lacking skills. He was lacking *fire*. From our very first deep-dive session, the signs were obvious. His 360 feedback was brutal—but accurate. And when I asked how it landed, he exhaled like the wind had been knocked out of him.

"I just don't feel anything here anymore," he said.

That was the moment I knew that Greg wasn't broken. He was burned out and on autopilot. His team felt it, too.

Disconnection at the top doesn't stay at the top—it trickles down and poisons everything below it.

We didn't start with systems or strategy, but with Greg's *why.* It was uncomfortable work at first, but slowly, session by session, Greg started reconnecting with the things that actually mattered to him:

- Building a team that thrived
- Contributing to the bank's success
- Making a meaningful impact on the lives of his employees

Once Greg remembered what he was fighting for, everything shifted. His energy returned. His creativity exploded. And most importantly—his leadership style transformed.

He stopped passively reacting and started purposely building culture. He set up accountability systems that weren't just about pressure—they were about support. He led with honesty, empathy, and clarity. He showed up. *Fully.*

People who were ready to quit started staying late to collaborate. Hostile meetings turned dynamic. That department didn't just bounce back—it turned a corner and became a flagship team inside the bank.

Greg didn't get better because someone handed him a new title or gave him a new team. He got better because he got honest. He faced his burnout, reconnected with his purpose, and made the *decision* to lead from within. It was a decision that changed *everything* around him. (Because that's what real self-motivation does.)

Would you rather follow a leader who moves with purpose—or one who's just going through the motions?

We both know the answer.

So here's the real question: Which one are you becoming?

Breaking Down the Motivation That Moves You

Real motivation isn't some fluctuating feeling that fades with friction. It doesn't show up when it's easy and disappear when it's not. It doesn't care about noise, obstacles, or how good your playlist is. Our style of motivation has crap to do—and it stays focused on that crap no matter what.

It's not fleeting like the rush you get from a killer speech or a perfect workout. Those moments are cool—but they don't last. Real motivation runs deeper. It's grounded in something more substantial and built on three principles: Discipline. Consistency. Restraint.

These three are what give a solid leader their edge. When you carry them, you separate yourself, stop being reactive, and stop chasing highs. Instead, you show up every single day—no matter what life throws your way.

This kind of "MADE motivation" is about honoring the commitments you made to yourself (and your team), long after the excitement of setting those goals has worn off.

Let's go back to Greg. When we first met, he was living in the land of traditional motivation. His drive (when it was there) came in bursts. He'd push for a quarter, then fade out. He'd get inspired by a new idea or a corporate campaign, ride that for a while, and then crash into the same wall. That's hype for you. It promises everything, delivers little, and vanishes when things get hard.

Discipline: Keeping Your Word When No One's Watching

In my work with Greg, discipline started small. He made one commitment—to reconnect with his team every morning, no matter how drained or distracted he felt. Some days he wanted to cancel. Some mornings he'd open his laptop and stare at the meeting link, wondering what he'd even say. But no matter how he felt or what else was going on professionally or personally, he showed up anyway.

Discipline is a decision to show up. It's loyalty to yourself, your future self, and those around you. You either keep your word, or you prove you can't be trusted—not even by you. Every time Greg honored that small commitment, he rebuilt trust.

Consistency: Turning Effort into Momentum

At first, Greg's team didn't completely buy the "new" him. They'd seen leaders rediscover their *whys* and recommit before. So he didn't try to convince them. He just kept showing up. Day after day, one meeting at a time, one follow-up at a time, one uncomfortable conversation at a time. Slowly, their skepticism shifted into curiosity, then into trust.

Consistency quietly builds proof. You win because you show up when others quit. That's how momentum is made—one small, steady act at a time.

Restraint: Starving Distraction, Feeding Purpose

The final pillar of MADE Motivation is restraint—the ability to say "no" when everything in you wants to chase comfort or distraction.

In his early burnout days, Greg chased easy wins. He'd spend hours lost in reports that didn't matter or get caught up solving problems that weren't his to solve. It felt productive, but it wasn't progress.

Once he reconnected to his "why," he stopped feeding every fire that popped up and started protecting his focus. He learned to pause before reacting, to think before fixing, to choose progress over motion. Through that restraint, his team became sharper, calmer, more accountable. They mirrored his focus.

Regular motivation is a spark—it burns hot, then fades. MADE Motivation is the fire you build from that spark. It's disciplined, consistent, restrained, and self-sustaining. It doesn't depend on a perfect Monday, a new year, or an external push. It's built from the inside out. You stay committed—even when the facts don't add up. And the facts? They run deep.

FACT 1: Your friends are going to quit.
The people who started with you won't all finish with you. Some will lose motivation, some will settle, and some will even resent your commitment because it makes them feel guilty about their own lack of effort. Keep going anyway. Sometimes doing great things means doing them alone.

FACT 2: People will call you crazy and say you're taking your goal too seriously.
That's because most people only give 50 percent and can't stand watching someone give 100 percent. They'll mock what they don't understand—until you succeed. Then they'll ask how you did it.

FACT 3: You will feel like an impostor.
There will be days when you question whether you're even capable of reaching your goal. Doubt will creep in, and your mind will try to convince you that you're not good enough. Ignore it and keep moving.

FACT 4: Life is going to hit you at the worst possible time.
Right when you get momentum, expect setbacks—financial stress, family emergencies, exhaustion, self-doubt. They're not excuses to stop. They're tests to see how bad you really want it.

FACT 5: You will be tempted to take the easy way out.
There will be shortcuts, distractions, and comfort zones begging you to return. The easy way is crowded with people who never finish. The hard way is where transformation happens.

FACT 6: No one is coming to save you.
Basic motivation fades. Support fades. Even encouragement from others will fade. At some point, it's just you, your goal, and your decision to keep pushing or quit.

FACT 7: You will have to sacrifice.
Time, comfort, distractions—something has to give. The question is whether you'll sacrifice *for* your goal or sacrifice your goal.

FACT 8: You will want to quit.
Not once, but many times. The difference between success and failure isn't talent or luck—it's whether you stop when it gets hard or push through anyway.

Most folks are ruled by their moods—fickle, fragile, always shifting. And those moods betray our desire to win, derailing the mission.

But the best leaders know better. Motivation has zero to do with your mood. It's about your mission. That's why your first job is to find your "why"—that deep, unshakable reason you chose to lead in the first place. Without it, you'll crumble the second life punches back.

Why do you lead? Why are you here?

Is it the title? The paycheck? The status? Or is it because you're dead serious about making an impact—and leaving it better than you found it?

If your answer feels hollow, don't panic. But don't ignore it either. Motivation must be rooted in *radical self-awareness*. Once you're honest about your why, you can begin deepening it into something that's sustainable instead of shallow. But if your why isn't clear and personal, you'll fall into the same trap everyone else does: burnout, disengagement, bitterness, and blame.

The world doesn't need more people chasing promotions. It needs people who've done the *inner work* to move with clarity and lead from purpose. And if your why doesn't shake you up, it's not big enough. Get real with yourself. Get raw. And lead like it matters—*because it does.*

Activity: Questions to Discover Your *Why*

Before we go any further, let's slow down for a moment and re-assess our why, just like Greg did. Discovering your why isn't busywork—it's the foundation supporting your journey to becoming MADE and learning how to win by 100. Take a breath, take your time, and be honest with yourself as you work through these questions.

1. What is one core value that you deeply believe in and would never compromise, even if it made leadership harder? Reflect on why this value is important and how it shapes your decisions.

2. When you think about the moments you felt most alive or fulfilled in your leadership journey, what were you doing, and why did it matter to you? Look for patterns or themes in these moments to uncover what drives you.

3. What kind of legacy do you want to leave as a leader? Picture your leadership's long-term impact on your family, your team, or your organization. How does this vision align with your actions today?

4. What frustrates or angers you most about the world, your organization, or your industry, and how could your leadership help solve it? Passion often hides in the problems we feel most compelled to fix.

5. What values or purpose are you willing to stand by, even if no one else knows? If all the external rewards (titles, money, recognition) disappeared tomorrow, what would still drive you to lead? Answering this can help separate superficial motivation from your true purpose.

4

Motivation – Dials, Switches, and Needs

I was leading an HG Leadership Seminar at Bangor Savings Bank—a company that's earned serious respect, consistently topping JD Power rankings. Midway through, a participant named Jeannie Stanhope said something that stopped me cold.

"I'm a dial person, not a switch person."

That was it. No extra context. No dramatic pause. Just that line. I felt it in my chest like a punch. It hit because I knew exactly what she meant. And more than that—I knew most people needed to hear it.

Since that moment, I've seen it everywhere. In teams. In coaching. In families. You've got two types of people: *dial people* and *switch people.*

Dial people warm up slowly. Like a thermostat. Like a volume knob. Their energy adjusts in degrees. They ramp up. Shift gears. Adapt. Sometimes slow to start—but consistent.

Switch people are binary. On or off. All-in or ghost mode. When they're on, they burn hot. Intense. Unstoppable. But when they're off? Good luck getting a spark. The light's out. The engine's cold.

The part many leaders miss is that you shouldn't try to lead *dials* and *switches* the same way. Good leaders don't force people into one mold. They figure out what makes their people move—and then meet them there. Some need coaxing. Others need a jolt. Some need time and space to simmer. Others need a reason to flip on.

Ask my wife—she'll tell you without hesitation: I'm a switch. When I'm on, *I'm on*. Full throttle. Smiles, handshakes, kissing babies (even the ugly ones), connecting with everyone in the room. I don't just flip the switch—I *am* the switch. *(I'm a switch person.)*

But when I'm off? Game over. I disappear. Doesn't matter who's calling or what's happening. My energy's gone. My mind goes quiet. My soul taps out.

Truth is, I'm wired for introversion. Always have been. But my work? My mission? It pulls extroversion out of me every single day. And I give it—gladly. But it costs me. Because when my tank runs dry, it's not a slow fade . . . it's a full shutdown.

I used to feel guilty about that. Like I should have more gas in the tank. Like I should be able to stretch it longer, stay on for just one more person. But then I realized something that changed everything:

Being a switch isn't a flaw—it's a feature.

And thank God for a life partner who gets that. She doesn't judge it. She doesn't try to fix it. She gives me space to recharge. She knows when the switch flips off, it's not defiance—it's recovery. It's survival. It's *reset.*

Maybe you needed to hear that. Maybe you've been burning yourself out trying to be a switch when you're built like a dial. Or maybe you've been leading dials and wondering why they don't "light up" on demand.

This isn't about changing people. It's about *understanding* them. Because self-awareness isn't a soft skill. It's survival.

Whether you're leading a team or just trying to lead yourself, growth starts when you stop pretending to be someone else and finally understand *you*. Dial or switch, you've got to know how you move. How you reset. How you recharge. That's the only way to lead with real stamina and real impact.

Self-Motivated Leadership Versus Externally-Motivated Leadership

The data in the below chart make it clear that self-motivated leaders are the preferred leaders of the day. To be self-motivated, and to coach others toward it, you need to understand how human motivation works.

To lead with impact, you've got to understand what actually makes people tick. Not just what they *say* drives them—but what moves them deep down. Great leadership isn't about task lists and timelines. It's about knowing how to pull the best out of people when everything's on the line.

And before you lead others, you better know what's moving you. That's where Maslow steps in—and that's where we're heading next.

	Self-Motivated Leader	Non-Self-Motivated Leader
Drive	Internally driven by purpose	Relies on external pushes
Impact on Team	Inspires commitment and enthusiasm	Models disengagement and lack of initiative
Handling of Challenges	Resilient and proactive	More easily discouraged, reactive
Consistency	Steady and reliable	Inconsistent and unfocused
Long-Term Outcome	Lasting impact on team culture and performance	Short-lived impact, struggles with turnover

Maslow's Theory: The Ladder of Human Motivation

Every great leader eventually has to ask the same question: *What really moves people?*

Not what excites them for a week, but what sustains their drive for years.

That's where Abraham Maslow comes in. Long before leadership books and motivational speakers filled shelves, Maslow was studying the same question—what fuels human motivation at its core? In 1943, he published his breakthrough paper, "A Theory of Human Motivation," and later expanded it in *Motivation and Personality* (1954). What he proposed wasn't just a theory—it was a truth bomb that gave us a blueprint for understanding how humans grow, lead, and thrive.

Maslow showed that people aren't simply chasing random wants. We're climbing a ladder of needs, each one building on the one before it:

- Survival: Food, water, air. Basic life support.
- Safety: Protection, security, stability. Both physical and emotional.
- Love and Belonging: Real connection—family, friendships, community.
- Esteem: Real respect for yourself and feeling respected by others.
- Self-Actualization: Becoming the best, truest version of who you were meant to be.

Miss a step, and everything above it shakes. Nail each one, and you finally build the kind of life—and leadership—that stands strong.

Maslow was basically shouting at the world: You can't chase your dreams if you're too busy worrying about your next meal. And here's the scary part that modern research confirms—in today's workplace too many people *never get past survival mode.* They're not thinking about growth, leadership, or purpose. They're just trying to make it through the day without breaking.

Decades after its introduction, Maslow's theory remains one of the most effective frameworks for understanding *what drives people.* If you're serious about being a great leader, you must grasp these fundamentals, so we will take a deeper dive here. You'll find that Maslow's philosophy will not only redefine your leadership approach but also set you apart as the kind of leader people will always remember and appreciate.

Picture Maslow's Theory as a five-rung ladder, where each rung represents a crucial layer of human needs. At the base, we find the essentials for survival—procreation, food, water, sleep, and shelter. At the very top, lies self-actualization, the pinnacle of human potential, where individuals experience deep fulfillment and inner peace.

▲ **Self-Actualization**–Becoming your best self (creativity, problem-solving, purpose)

↑ **Esteem Needs**–Confidence, achievement, respect from others

↑ **Love & Belonging**–Friendships, family, relationships, sense of connection

↑ **Safety Needs**–Security, stability, financial health, personal safety

↑ **Physiological Needs**–Food, water, air, sleep, shelter (basic survival)

Starting at the bottom (Physiological Needs), human motivation climbs this ladder step-by-step. The idea is simple but profound: if the foundational needs aren't met, it's much harder to summon the energy or focus to engage with the higher levels. For example, try developing a groundbreaking business strategy while your stomach growls from hunger or while you're losing sleep over job insecurity. It's nearly impossible, and Maslow's framework explains why.

The theory reflects what you've likely experienced firsthand: when the basics aren't secure, everything else takes a back seat.

Maslow's hierarchy offers a real-world blueprint for motivation. The top shelf (self-actualization) is always more "expensive" than the bottom shelf (basic needs), making the climb from survival to thriving a natural progression, not just an idea in a textbook.

Great leaders recognize this. They don't waste time pushing high-level aspirations on people still struggling with the fundamentals. Instead, they remove unseen barriers, creating the conditions for real growth—so everyone has the chance to climb.

And Maslow's theory isn't just about individuals—it plays out in *every* organization, too. Let's break down each level, from basic survival needs to self-actualization, and examine what they look like in the workplace. Along the way, I'll highlight some modern organizational failures tied to these levels—some of which may challenge the way you think.

1. Biological and Physiological Needs

These are easy.

They're the "must-haves" for basic survival: *oxygen, food, water, reproduction, rest.* Without these, any person, culture, or society would surely falter. In the workplace, this translates into fair wages and reasonable working conditions. You can't expect an employee to be motivated by company goals if they can't afford the basics on their salary.

Imagine this: Carla clocks in for her shift at 9 a.m., already carrying the weight of the day. Not just the workday—the real day. Rent's due. The fridge is running low. The electric bill's still sitting on the counter, unopened—not because she forgot, but because she already knows what it says.

No surprises. No cushion. No backup plan. Every dollar matters. And as Ben Franklin put it, "time is money"—so every minute of her workday counts. She *needs* this shift.

But then—her phone buzzes.

The school nurse.

Her stomach tightens. *Not today. Please, not today,* she prays under her breath as she answers the call.

"Carla, your child has a fever. Can you come pick him up, please?"

Carla knew the fever was low grade when she dropped him off that morning, praying he'd get through the day. She knows it's just a minor virus, but she also already knows what the call means for her paycheck.

No backup. No childcare. No paid time off.

She's stretched thin as it is, even juggling a second job just to keep the Wi-Fi on so her kids can do their homework.

She looks around the workplace, calculating. If she leaves, she risks losing hours she can't afford to miss. If she stays, she risks being seen as a bad mother. Either way, *Carla loses.*

She exhales slowly, steadying herself, trying to answer the question of the moment … clock out or push through? Neither choice is fair. But she doesn't have the luxury of fairness—*only survival.*

For working parents like Carla, even *lunch* might be a luxury they must sometimes quietly forgo. So, when colleagues invite her to join them for a noontime meal, she brushes it off with a casual excuse: "Oh, I've got a Zoom meeting at 12:15; y'all go ahead." Beneath her calm response lies a quiet dignity, masking the relentless pressures of simply trying to make it work, day by day, or even hour by hour.

Societally, we understand that a lunchless school day should never be a reality for kids. Thankfully, nowadays, most school districts provide free breakfast and lunch for students from struggling homes, ensuring they can focus on learning instead of being derailed by the discomfort of hunger. Programs like these give kids like Carla's the energy to hope, to dream, to aim for more than just *getting by*.

But what about the parents of those free lunch kids? Those children have moms and dads who head off to work each day with their own empty stomach, bracing themselves for the grind. They push through without a meal, without a break, and often without a moment to catch their breath.

If you believe this sounds farfetched, it isn't. According to 2022 Pew Research study, one in four employed U.S. parents had struggled to afford food or housing in the past year. Sadly, this is a grim reality, even for those working full-time jobs. And if you didn't already know, I'll tell you: if Carla has to choose who will go hungry—her *or* her kids—it will be her, *every single time.*

The same system that feeds children like Carla's often overlooks Carla herself, leaving working parents to endure long hours fueled only by their resolve to make ends meet. These parents show up every day, despite what they lack. And sometimes, no one recognizes what they're sacrificing.

Hungry parents aren't thinking about how to go *above and beyond* at work. According to Maslow's theory, they're focused on *surviving the day*. Their minds drift—not to their boss's plea for ideas and higher outputs, but to the gnawing hunger in their guts and the looming question of dinner, knowing their kids' free-school-lunch-filled bellies won't last until bedtime. They're in survival mode, operating on fumes. How can we expect an employee to thrive at work when they're fighting just to make it to tomorrow?

Additionally, consider work schedules that deny people enough time for rest (another basic need). Expecting someone to be innovative or team-oriented when they're chronically sleep-deprived is setting them—and the company—up for failure. Basic pay and conditions are non-negotiable if you're trying to build a productive, motivated workforce.

MADE Leadership Action

- Review your team's compensation and work hours.
- Are they paid enough to meet their basic needs? Are they stretched thin by unreasonable shifts?
- Pay close attention to the people in your organization—often, there are subtle cues that employees are struggling to get by.
- Show your team that you care by addressing these foundational needs first.

2. Safety and Security Needs

Safety in the workplace is more than a box to check or a fire drill to schedule. It's a feeling. A visceral, deeply rooted sense of security that touches every part of a person's experience. A solid leader understands that safety has layers—physical, emotional, and psychological—and that true leadership means addressing *all three.*

Employees need more than a safe environment; they need to feel safe in it. And yes, there's a difference. You can have all the policies in the world and still leave people feeling exposed, uncertain, and undervalued. Good leaders recognize this gap. Great leaders close it!

Physical safety is where it starts. If your employees are worried about slipping on the factory floor, breathing in harmful fumes, or working with outdated equipment, they're not thinking about how to innovate or grow your business. Survival mode overrides ambition 100 percent of the time.

Solid leaders don't wait for an incident to act. They anticipate risks, prioritize safety, and create a culture where employees trust that their well-being matters—not just to the organization but to their leader, as well. Good leaders have safety policies. Great leaders create safe spaces!

The pandemic taught us this: *uncertainty kills trust.* Employees can't focus on thriving when they're stuck worrying if their job will disappear tomorrow. Solid leaders don't let silence create a void for fear to grow. They keep their people in the loop. They're transparent about the organization's challenges and victories. Great leaders know that when employees trust in the stability of their role, they stop looking over their shoulders and start looking forward.

Good leaders inform their teams. Great leaders empower them to see the bigger picture!

In today's world, leadership extends beyond work hours. Employees don't clock out of stress, anxiety, or burnout just because the day is done. MADE leaders understand that people aren't just workers—they're *whole humans*. They encourage balance, provide resources, and model the behavior they want to see in others. A leader who burns out quietly drags their team down with them. A leader who prioritizes well-being shows their team it's okay to do the same. Good leaders hope their team is okay. Great leaders make sure that they are!

The Growing Weight of Psychological Safety

Here's where great leaders set themselves apart. Physical safety is visible. Job security is measurable. *But psychological safety?* It's intangible, yet its impact is profound. This is the difference between employees speaking up or staying silent, between bringing their best ideas or holding them back.

Psychological safety is about more than avoiding conflict or criticism—it's about creating *trust*. It's the assurance that someone can share their ideas, concerns, or mistakes without fear of ridicule or retaliation. In workplaces where this is absent, innovation stalls, collaboration weakens, and motivation dries up.

Imagine working in a place where you're afraid to make mistakes. Where a missed step feels like a landmine, ready to blow up your credibility. You're not growing there; you're surviving. Great leaders don't let that fear take root. They cultivate cultures where vulnerability is a strength and honesty is a given.

And it's important to communicate about psychological safety, too. You must talk about it openly. Just because you *are* a safe space for people, it doesn't mean that they *know it* and *feel it.* A person is only as safe as they feel they are.

I once caught an episode of a daytime court TV show—the kind where the cases are petty, but the drama is always top tier. Admittedly, I love a good episode of *Judge Judy* or *Judge Mathis.* Maybe it's nostalgia—growing up, I spent countless afternoons with my great-grandmother, who rarely missed an episode of *The People's Court* way back in the Judge Wapner days.

But this episode? This one stuck with me. A woman was suing her neighbor over *a dog-related incident.* And in her defense, this wasn't just any dog—this was a Mastiff. And if you've ever seen a Mastiff, you know exactly what that means. These dogs aren't just big. They're enormous! Put a saddle on one, and people might mistake it for a horse.

The plaintiff claimed she was injured after a scuffle with her neighbor's massive Mastiff, and from the looks of it, this case was going to be open and shut. I mean, they even brought the dog into the courtroom for dramatic effect. It just stood there, tongue out, drooling—its size alone made it look guilty as charged.

The defendant, of course, swore up and down that her dog was a gentle giant—a big ol' baby who wouldn't hurt a fly. (But that's what they all say, isn't it?)

As the case unfolded, it turned out . . . she was telling the truth. The Mastiff didn't *bite the woman.* Didn't *lunge at her.* Didn't even *bark at her.* So what really happened?

The plaintiff admitted she had a deep, paralyzing fear of big dogs. So when she unexpectedly found herself on the same side of the street as the lawfully harnessed and totally tamed Mastiff, her mind (and fear) went into overdrive.

Her eyes locked onto the big dog, waiting—*expecting*—an attack. She saw it play out in her head: the heavy beast lunging, teeth sinking into her flesh, pain ripping through her body … the months (maybe years) of agony, hospital bills, surgeries. She saw it all unfolding.

But the Mastiff just stood there—cooler than Snoopy sipping a slushy. Lawfully leashed. Calm. Tail wagging like it knew the joke.

But that didn't stop the woman from panicking. She flipped out like a somersault trying to escape the attack that never came. She scrambled to sidestep the impending danger that didn't exist.

And in that chaos, she stepped wrong, suffering a sprained ankle, broken pinky, and dislocated elbow.

The dog wasn't the problem. The plaintiff's *fear* was the problem.

As a MADE leader, you're a safe presence for your team—not because you say so, but because they feel it. Sure, your title may make you the "big dog" in the room, but the way you carry yourself matters more. Like a gentle Mastiff—large, respected, but approachable—you lead with calm authority, fairness, and even a little warmth.

Still, don't ignore this truth: *not everyone sees you that way*. Some team members may flinch, shut down, or hold back—not because of *you*, but because of who came before you. Maybe they were burned, belittled, or blindsided by a leader who wore the same collar. So when you walk into the room, they don't just see *you*—they see every boss who ever barked, chased them, or bit them.

That's not your fault, but it *is* your responsibility. Being a great leader means understanding that psychological safety isn't just built by your actions—it's shaped by their experience. And if you want trust, you've got to earn it on their terms, not yours.

When people feel unsafe at work—even if the danger is not real but merely *perceived*—they start playing small. They sidestep conflict, hold back ideas, and protect themselves instead of participating. Not because they're weak, but because they don't trust they won't get "bitten." And when trust is missing, teams don't grow—they survive. That's not a team dynamic. That's a trauma response. This is exactly what Maslow warned us about: without safety, you'll never achieve healthy relationships or esteem.

Psychological safety isn't just about being nice or ethical—it's about making safety undeniably clear. That means communicating it with consistency, integrity, and follow-through until every team member knows it's safe to speak up, show up, and grow.

A good dog might wag its tail, but a great leader wags their transparency, trustworthiness, and fairness in a way that leaves no room for doubt. Below are some tips to help you build this kind of trust and ensure your team never awkwardly steps off the corporate curb for their own unfounded fears.

How MADE Leaders Build Psychological Safety

1. Transparency Builds Bridges: Good leaders communicate when they must. Great leaders keep their teams in the loop—always. Employees can't feel secure if they're left in the dark.
2. Vulnerability Starts at the Top: Admitting mistakes doesn't weaken a leader's authority—it strengthens it.

When leaders own their flaws, employees feel safe to own theirs too.

3. Recognition Fuels Confidence: Acknowledge ideas, effort, and progress—not just results. Great leaders know that when people feel seen, they feel safe to try again.
4. Clarity Defuses Doubt: Ambiguity creates anxiety. Great leaders set clear expectations, so employees know what success looks like and how to achieve it.
5. Toxicity Has No Place: Great leaders shut down disrespect, bullying, or passive-aggressive behavior the second it shows up. Toxicity thrives in silence, and silence is a leadership failure.

MADE Leadership Action

- Mental health support, flexible schedules, fair wages—these aren't extras, they're essentials.
- Implement a "no-surprise" policy to normalize transparency and build trust.
- When employees are in the loop and know where they stand, they feel safer and more valued. Communicate openly, maintain consistent protocols, and show that you're committed to their stability and growth.
- Go beyond surface questions. Ask how employees are doing in their roles and in their lives. Then, act on what you learn.

3. Love and Belonging Needs

Love and belonging aren't soft concepts—they're human needs. According to Maslow's hierarchy, once people have their basic physical and psychological needs met, they seek connection. That includes acceptance, inclusion, and meaningful relationships. In a leadership context, this matters more than most leaders realize. When people don't feel like they belong, they disconnect, underperform, or leave. But when leaders create environments where people feel seen, valued, and connected, teams don't just function—they flourish. Love and belonging aren't luxuries in the workplace; they're leadership responsibilities.

In today's business world, you can't talk about the third rung of Maslow's hierarchy—Love and Belonging—without bumping into the corporate buzzword that's dominated the last few years: DEIB (Diversity, Equity, Inclusion, and Belonging).

I didn't come here to stir controversy. But if we're going to talk candidly about what it means to feel like you belong at work, we have to go there—and we have to go deep, because it's been a major issue and it desperately needs clarity.

DEIB was introduced as the modern answer to Maslow's idea of relationship and connection at work. But before I show you why Maslow's framework is more than enough, I've got to tell you why DEIB—at least in its current form—isn't working.

Let's clear the air right now: This is *not* an attack on diversity. This is *not* a takedown of equity. This is *not* a rejection of inclusion or belonging. I'm on the record saying that I support every one of those principles.

Fiercely. But there's a big difference between *values* and *initiatives*.

What we've seen in DEIB over the past few years isn't bad intent. It's bad structure. It's policy without practicality. Purpose without clarity. In too many places, it's been politicized, weaponized, and turned into something it was never meant to be.

Here's an uncomfortable truth:

If love and belonging are real—they don't need to be enforced. They don't need a policy or a program to exist. They show up because they *are*, not because someone demanded them.

Here's another one:

You don't owe everyone access.

And one more (since we're here):

You don't owe everyone respect either.

Let me break that last one down, because I know it probably ruffled some feathers.

We owe people the absence of disrespect—that's basic human decency. But respect? That's different. Respect is earned.

I've worked with (or tried to coach) people who, through their actions, proved they didn't deserve my respect. So I didn't give it. But I was *never* disrespectful.

That wasn't about *them*. That was about *me*. About the standard I hold for how I show up in the world. Organizations should be no different.

Love. Belonging. Access. Respect. You know what they all have in common in the corporate world? They're earned. Not handed out. Not owed. Not guaranteed. And they sure as heck aren't something you enforce with a policy. Because when you hand these out unearned, you don't build culture—you dilute it. You start a slow drip of diminishing returns on everything you're trying to create.

A healthy culture doesn't come from giving everyone a seat at the table. It comes from earning that seat—and knowing you've earned it.

This isn't about *exclusion.* This is about *elevation.*

When people *earn* love, belonging, access, and respect? They rise. And when they rise, the whole culture rises with them.

The Thermostat Rule: Why Balance Matters

Maslow's hierarchy shows us where to focus. Right there, dead center in the pyramid is Love and Belonging.

It's at the center because it's the clear core of human connection. The foundation of inclusion that doesn't divide or dictate. It doesn't need slogans. It needs leaders who understand this:

You can't legislate belonging. It's not a policy—it's a culture. Rules can mandate behavior, but they can't manufacture respect. The second we try to control emotions, it's not inclusion—it's manipulation. (And even good people don't like to be manipulated.)

You can't pretend the playing field is already level. Meritocracy only works when opportunities are real. And right now, they're not real for everyone.

Let's stop pretending that DEIB will save your culture. Let's stop acting like you can fix systemic issues with one all-hands training and a few PowerPoint slides. Real belonging isn't about perfection or comfort. It's not about handing out passes or walking on eggshells. It's about creating a space where people are respected, challenged, and empowered—even when that gets messy.

Real development isn't neat and orderly. Development and belonging are messy.

But both are worth it and require leadership. As leaders, our job isn't to coddle people or police every emotion. Our job is to build teams rooted in clarity, trust, and shared purpose. Maslow already gave us the blueprint. Let's stop building initiatives that drift from it—and start building cultures that live it.

Years ago, my wife and I settled a silent war in our bedroom.

I run hot.

She runs cold.

If we set the thermostat just for her, I'm sweating through the sheets. Set it for me, and she's reaching for a parka. The solution wasn't heat or AC—it was compromise. Not perfect comfort for either of us, but livable comfort for both.

That's leadership. Not tiptoeing around one group. Not steamrolling another. Real leadership is setting the temperature where most people can show up, do meaningful work, and still feel like they belong—without sacrificing the values that hold it all together.

You're not trying to make everyone happy. You're trying to build an environment that works. That's the job. Let's keep that in mind as we push forward.

The best leaders aren't out here waging ideological war. We're focused on impact. And the impact is clear—leadership without balance fails. Always.

Respect and fairness. Give people a real shot—without lowering the bar.

Challenge and growth. Nobody gets better through comfort alone.

Compromise and adaptability. Life is built in the gray. Learn to see it. Learn to speak it.

Love and Belonging: Maslow Got It Right

Maslow placed love and belonging right in the middle of his pyramid—not just physically, but functionally. It's the third rung, and the final one in what he called the *"deficiency needs"*—the ones that scream the loudest when they're missing from our lives.

You don't crave food most when you're full and satiated. You crave it when you're hungry or starving.

Same with belonging. When people feel isolated, excluded, or invisible, it's all they can think about. That need to be seen, heard, and known becomes consuming. And until it's addressed, productivity, creativity, and collaboration are all stuck in neutral.

Once survival and safety are met, people move toward connection. That's the shift from "I'm okay" to "Do I matter?"—and it's where leaders make the biggest difference.

But here's the catch: When belonging is over-engineered, forced, or politicized, it backfires. Instead of making people feel included, it pressures them to conform. That's not love or belonging. That's performance. That's fear. That's *artificial harmony.*

The Real Role of Leaders

As a leader, your role isn't to engineer belonging by force. It's to create conditions where belonging happens naturally. Through trust. Through clarity. Through mutual respect.

You're either fostering connection—or creating quiet isolation. There is no neutral setting.

The fastest way to fracture a culture? Chase belonging without boundaries. I've seen it firsthand—well-intentioned leaders trying to build inclusive spaces but doing it without clear expectations or structure. In the name of inclusion, they unintentionally create environments where accountability disappears, standards get blurred, and trust quietly erodes. That's not real inclusion. It's just some form of performative chaos.

To be clear, exclusion in years past did real damage. People were overlooked, silenced, and shut out of opportunities they'd earned. We don't ignore that. But inclusion without clarity brings a different kind of harm—one that's subtle, harder to name, but just as capable of killing culture from the inside out.

That's why we need to talk about this—frankly, directly, and without spin. And that's exactly what these next pages are for.

Case Study: When Belonging Backfires

Most organizations say they want inclusion. Fewer know how to create it. Even fewer survive the backlash when they try. I've worked with dozens of companies on DEIB. All meant well. A handful got it *basically* right. The rest? They alienated some of their best people—many without even knowing it. *Why?* Because the ones feeling isolated weren't allowed to say so. And that's the problem.

The DEIB pendulum didn't just swing. It snapped. And in too many places, it smacked good people in the mouth. After George Floyd. During the pandemic. Mid-political chaos. Corporate America didn't walk into DEIB—they sprinted. With slogans in hand and hashtags at the ready, companies charged forward to prove they were *"on the right side of history."* It felt righteous. Noble. Urgent. I was there for it. Called in by company after company to help "make culture more inclusive." And at the beginning, I was all in. I believed in it 100 percent.

Until I didn't.

There's a company in Maine I used to admire greatly. Big name. Strong brand. Solid values. I'd had my eye on them for years—thought we were destined to work together. So when a friend (we'll call her Kathy) invited me to co-facilitate a DEIB-related session, I jumped.

It felt like the perfect fit. Kathy was brilliant. I was ready. We designed a seminar on *Inclusive Leadership* that blended her DEIB expertise with my leadership development experience. I was excited. Energized. And exceedingly grateful.

But after just a few sessions, a pattern started to show up in our post-session recaps with the admin overseeing the work. Kathy got glowing reviews across the board. I got strong feedback, too—but there was always one barbed comment tucked inside the praise. Something I said or showed was "problematic." *Every. Single. Time.*

That word stuck with me. I've come to learn when something makes people uncomfortable, they often label it *"a problem."* But not everything that makes you uncomfortable is wrong. Sometimes, discomfort is just the first step toward growth—and that's exactly where real development begins.

One person in the first session found something I said "problematic." In a different session, one person flagged a stock image I used—yes, a Microsoft stock photo of a flower—as "suggestive." In another session, one person got offended when I spoke truthfully about leadership dynamics and referred to the findings of a seminal study. This was stuff I've studied and taught for decades without incident, using the same scenarios and stories, same data and examples, the same diction, and even the same jokes.

I wasn't careless with my words. I wasn't combative or provocative. I just told the truth—openly, respectfully, and with humility. I even led with this: "I'm not a DEIB expert. That's why Kathy is here. I'm here to learn from her alongside you while connecting the dots from the lessons in DEIB to lessons in leadership."

I made it clear I wasn't an expert but was willing to put myself on display to hopefully give others confidence to open up and engage in their own personal DEIB journey.

But none of that mattered. One person got uncomfortable. And it spread across the organization.

Since then, I've been recommended to that company—by at least four corporate partners and colleagues (that I *know* of)—for work I was built to do: leadership analysis, executive coaching, culture change, team development. But what have I heard from the company? *Crickets.*

Meanwhile, other consultants who quote my work—cite me in their slide decks, list my articles and interviews on their reference pages—they got hired there. While I didn't even get a call.

You know what that feels like? Like showing up to the table—heart open, hands clean—and still getting kicked out of the room. Not for doing harm. Not for breaking rules. But for breaking comfort.

One person's comfort.

What about my comfort?

I was the one standing there at the front of the room—openly, publicly, intentionally—putting my own vulnerability on the line. Willing to examine my own blind spots. Willing to get uncomfortable *first*, so others might feel safer doing the same. That was literally a known and stated goal. An intended reason for my presence in the project.

I wasn't to merely talk about inclusion—I was to model and demonstrate what it could look like to wrestle with it honestly. My goal was to name, out loud, the very things that get in a leader's way when they try to grow in this space.

I wasn't completely alone in supporting my approach. One staff member on the DEIB team there had been in every conversation, every session. He saw it all. And in the post-session debriefs, it was clear—he found the negative comments about me . . . *questionable.* He openly vouched for me, believing the criticism unwarranted and unreasonable. And not long after I was pushed out, I saw on LinkedIn that he'd moved on to different pastures.

I wish I was the only one with a story like this. But I'm not. There are good people—*great* people—being quietly pushed out of rooms that claim to be built on *belonging.*

Because they don't follow the exact same script.

Because they challenge a little too much.

Because their honesty makes the wrong person (or people) squirm.

Let's stop pretending that belonging is fragile. It's not. It's gritty. It's earned. It's honest. And it starts with this:

Let people bring their full selves.

Let them grow in real time.

And give them grace on the way up the ladder.

Because I still believe that almost everyone can belong. But no one will if we keep exiling the ones who speak the truth, respectfully and gracefully.

The Conference and the Conversation

Later that same year, I found myself at a Society for Human Resource Management (SHRM) conference on the coast of Rockport, Maine, taking in the salty air and sweeping ocean views at the breathtaking Samoset Resort. It was the kind of setting that begged for a neat pour of complex bourbon and a moment to ponder life's bigger questions.

That's when I spotted Dr. Jarik Conrad—author, HR heavyweight, and keynote speaker—sitting in the lobby. But instead of enjoying the view, he looked frustrated. The kind of frustration where a man sits still, but his mind is running a forty-yard dash.

I didn't know him, but I don't see a lot of other black men on the coast of Maine, and I was curious—not just to make a connection, but to be helpful if he needed. Something about his expression told me his mind wasn't on the ocean view, and I figured if I could do anything to make his day smoother, it was worth a conversation. I walked over.

"You good, bro?"

Turns out, he wasn't. His luggage was MIA, thanks to the fine folks in the baggage department at the airport. He told me that he was set to hit *the main stage* at this very conference the next day with nothing but the clothes on his back.

"Dang! That's a problem."

I felt bad for his situation. And since he and I were *about* the same size, I threw out a Hail Mary.

"Worst case, man, I've got an outfit for you."

I was ready to hand over my clothes for the next day—figured he needed them more than I did. I wasn't speaking; he was. Simple math.

"Or we can hit a TJ Maxx real quick. You know that place is like a poor man's Swiss Army knife."

He laughed, shook his head, and said, "Nah, I'm good—I talked to the airline, I think it'll all work out. But I appreciate it."

The next day, sure enough, I saw his name on the big stage lineup, and I made sure I was in the audience. And let me tell you—this guy was sharp. He didn't just present; he *commanded.* Jarik's speaking style isn't just delivery—*it's an experience*. He doesn't just tell stories; he pulls you in, making every word feel intentional, every pause build anticipation, and every point land with the kind of impact that sticks with you long after he's finished speaking. His insights on leadership, HR, and workplace culture weren't just informative—they were *real*, grounded in his own lived experience. I really enjoyed it.

When he wrapped up, he moved to a book signing table, where attendees could grab copies of his work and meet him in person. Naturally, the avid reader in me pushed me to the signing line. That's when the *real conversation* happened.

It was just a line of HR pros waiting for a signed book, talking shop. The conversation naturally turned to Jarik's session on DEIB—how it hit home, how it played out in their own workplaces. This talk wasn't a polished corporate script—it was raw. Unscripted. Real.

The challenge? It wasn't DEIB itself. It was *the execution*. These HR folks weren't questioning whether

DEIB mattered. They were wrestling with how the heck to pull it off in the middle of a chaotic labor market.

I love conversations like this, so I listened hard.

And the more I listened, the clearer it became—they weren't just struggling to build diverse teams. They were struggling to build *teams*, period. They didn't need quotas. They needed qualified people who could actually do their work. But the pipeline was bone dry. Turnover was gutting them. Leadership wasn't leading—they were triaging. Scrambling just to keep the wheels from flying off. Plus, all of this was happening at the peak of the pandemic—they were being told to "prioritize DEIB" while climbing a hiring mountain that was already near vertical.

DEIB wasn't being *rejected.* It was being *tested.*

I watched them circle the same unspoken truth, like execs playing corporate hot potato. Everyone could feel it. No one wanted to hold it. I waited to see if someone would break orbit and go deeper. But they just kept spinning. Because this was HR. This was corporate. The world where you say what's safe, what's polished, what *won't* get you in trouble.

But I wasn't in HR. I was just a consultant checking out the scene. Trying to see what's on the horizon for modern corporate participants. I wasn't there to play it so safe. So, I just said *the thing* out loud.

"But merit, right?" I offered, with a half-smile, looking around at the faces. "It's still important to make sure you get the right people, right? I mean . . . that's the goal in hiring, right? Getting people that can do the job. Right?"

Even though I posed it like it was halfway a question, somehow it still hit like a stun grenade. The faces on these folks when I said that—you'd think I'd flipped over the snack table.

I wasn't trying to be provocative. I just said the thing everyone was dancing around—the thing sitting in the center of that HR huddle like a six-hundred-pound gorilla.

After a few seconds of silence, I followed up my own question with my opinion on the matter.

"Companies should never sacrifice their standards in the name of DEIB or anything else," I said. "But at the same time, no employee should ever feel like they're second to anyone else because of who they are. That's the real tension, right? Not DEIB *or* merit—but figuring out how to honor both, without compromising either. *Right?*"

I paused. Took a breath.

I'd made up my mind that I wasn't saying another word until someone else chimed in. Slowly, I watched some body language shift. Some eyes sharpen. Some arms uncross. But still no one spoke.

Eventually, I caved: "I think we're capable of walking and chewing gum at the same time. We can do both. *Right*?"

And just like that—the air finished shifting.

People leaned in. Nodded. Some even exhaled, like I'd just said the words they'd been holding inside for too long. (And let me remind you—these were HR professionals.)

I wanted to show these HR leaders something simple: When discomfort gets mislabeled as harm, growth shuts down. And when one or two uncomfortable voices can silence the room, that's not inclusion—that's control. And in the name of inclusion, what you end up creating is exclusion.

Defining Inclusion: Chase One Rabbit

Confucius once said, "He who chases two rabbits catches none."

Mike Strout, a retired CHRO at Zildjian Company and one of my sharpest HR mentors, gave me the corporate version: "In leadership, no matter what you do you're going to piss some people off. Just make sure you piss off the right people."

Mike wasn't being flippant—he was being *real*. Leadership isn't about pleasing everyone. And inclusion? That's where the rubber really meets the road.

The best leaders don't define inclusion with buzzwords or blanket statements. They define it with clarity and conviction. As Max De Pree said, "The first job of a leader is to define reality." And the reality is this: inclusion rooted in Maslow's idea of love and belonging works—not because it's trendy, but because it's timeless. Respect, dignity, connection—those values outlast every corporate wave.

When companies chase *every* unique experience or try to accommodate *every* voice equally, they don't build stronger teams—they build confusion. Complexity seems inclusive, but it's often alienating. When everything becomes a priority, *nothing is.* That's why Maslow's framework matters: it brings us back to the basics. Human needs. Shared values. A simple truth—people thrive where they feel seen, respected, and useful. And that only happens when leaders pick the right rabbit.

MADE leaders don't chase every idea. They don't let a single voice rewrite the room. They create structure and consistency—environments where *almost everyone* can thrive, even if *no one* is 100 percent comfortable all the time.

That's not easy. That's not trendy.

But it's the only kind of leadership that truly lasts.

So pick a rabbit.

And happy hunting!

MADE Leadership Action

- Hold Real Check-Ins, Not Box-Ticks. Create space for honest, human conversations—especially in remote or hybrid teams. Don't just check in—tune in. Ask what's working, what's not, and where connection is missing.
- Break Silos. Build Bridges. Push for cross-team collaboration—not because it looks good, but because it fuels culture. Celebrate team wins publicly and loudly. Show people they're not just doing tasks—they're part of something bigger.
- Listen Without Fear or Filters. Offer an anonymous channel where people can speak freely about cultural initiatives—especially DEIB. Not just to check a box, but to truly understand how the message is landing. And when they speak? Listen like it matters. Because it does.
- Lead with Your Whole Self. Model vulnerability and authenticity—not as a performance, but as a pattern. When leaders go first, others follow. MADE leaders don't just allow openness—they normalize it.
- Make Belonging Tangible. Share stories that matter. Give real gratitude. Look people in the eye (or the camera) and make sure they know: I see you. I hear you. You matter here.

- Protect the Mission from Extremes. Love and belonging shouldn't be weaponized. Watch for ideological drift that hijacks your culture. Inclusion isn't making one group ultra-comfortable while pushing another to the edge. If one group's comfort requires another's silence, that's not belonging—that's imbalance. Fix it.

4. Esteem Needs

As individuals ascend upward in Maslow's hierarchy of needs, they move from addressing basic needs deficiencies to pursuing self-fulfillment and growth. Esteem is the bridge between these two realms—a pivotal point where individuals crave recognition, competence, and respect. Great leaders understand that meeting esteem needs is not just about recognition; it's about consistently nurturing a culture where people feel valued and capable.

This is where MADE aligns beautifully with Maslow's framework, particularly with *Growth Motivators.*

Maslow divided human needs into two categories: Deficiency Motivators and Growth Motivators. Deficiency Motivators drive people to address what's lacking—like food, safety, or belonging. These needs are universal; everyone aspires to them when they feel deficient. For example, a lack of psychological safety might push an employee to seek a workplace where they feel secure.

But growth motivators are different. They arise, not from scarcity, but from aspiration and ambition.

Esteem, the first of the growth motivators, is less about survival and more about thriving. It appeals to individuals who naturally aim higher, those with a true spirit of leadership. Great leaders recognize that growth motivators are not for everyone; they inspire people who desire to achieve, contribute, engage, and grow.

Case Study: Rebuilding the Leadership Pipeline at Haley Ward

Post-COVID, something fundamental shifted. Employees across industries started choosing peace over promotions. Family over frenzy. Simplicity over status. And while that's not wrong (in fact, it's healthy), it left growing firms with a serious challenge: a disappearing leadership pipeline.

Firms like Haley Ward—a fast-growing, employee-owned engineering and environmental consulting firm—found themselves at an inflection point in 2023. Growth was strong, fueled by a series of smart acquisitions. But inside the organization, the signs of strain were growing clearer: high-potential talent wasn't stepping up. Managers were burning out. And a widening gap had formed between opportunity and ambition.

This wasn't about skill shortages. The technical talent was there. What was missing was drive—specifically, the kind of internal motivation needed to take on leadership in a post-pandemic world.

When I first sat down with Denis St. Peter (CEO) and Travis Noyes (COO and Executive VP), they didn't sugarcoat it. They were already seeing the issue clearly and asking the right questions. That conversation led to the introduction of the MADE system—not as a one-time training, but as a cultural development shift focused on *self-leadership*.

The system works because it's built around one truth: All motivation is self-motivation.

You can't push people into leadership with titles or bonuses anymore. That playbook is outdated. What works now is helping people find their *why*—and building a culture where that *why* can grow. That's where Maslow's hierarchy of needs becomes critical.

Through structured work on Motivation, Assessment, Declaration, and Evaluation, Haley Ward didn't just tell employees to lead—they gave them the tools and space to choose it.

One standout example came from Dean Temple, a gifted senior architect who had long avoided higher-level leadership roles. After participating in the HG Leadership Seminar and engaging with the MADE framework, his mindset shifted, and he declared his readiness for new opportunities at higher ranks.

"I used to think leadership wasn't for me," Dean said. "But once I realized how much my work actually shaped the bigger picture—and how much my teammates needed me—it all clicked. I didn't need a new title. I needed a new perspective."

That shift—from resistance to ownership—rippled across teams.

With the system in motion, the culture at Haley Ward began to shift in real ways. Initiative increased. Dependency on senior leaders decreased. Project workloads balanced out. Managers stopped asking, "Why won't they step up?" and started asking, "How are we helping them *want* to?"

The firm moved from managing performance to *developing people.* From delegation to *development.* From pushing leaders forward to *pulling potential upward.* And Haley Ward is now better positioned to grow from within.

Not because people were told to lead—but because they chose to.

Why Esteem Matters in MADE Leadership

1. It Creates Self-Motivated Teams: When people feel valued and competent, they're more likely to take initiative and *own* their roles.
2. It Builds Trust and Loyalty: Consistent recognition fosters a sense of belonging and alignment with organizational goals.
3. It Fuels Growth: Esteem isn't about fluff; it's about creating an environment where people are driven to exceed expectations and stretch their potential.

Application Story: How a MADE Leader Addresses Esteem Needs!

Now that we understand why esteem matters, let me share Natalie's story.

Natalie, a newly promoted senior project manager at a mid-sized tech firm in the southeastern USA, had just been entrusted with her first major assignment in her elevated role. It was a career milestone, and as someone who has coached her since 2019, I couldn't have been prouder. Stepping into her new position, Natalie was eager to prove herself, but as with any promotion, the stakes felt higher, and her confidence was still solidifying.

The challenge before her was substantial: she was to lead a complex overhaul of the company's internal CRM system. It was a high-stakes project requiring coordination across teams, managing tight deadlines, and tackling technical obstacles. Natalie approached the task with determination and creativity, knowing this was her opportunity to establish herself as a firm leader.

Her efforts were nothing short of extraordinary. The project streamlined operations and were projected to save the company hundreds of thousands of dollars over the next decade—the kind of outcome that should impress any executive team or board. Yet when the project wrapped, Natalie's sense of accomplishment was overshadowed by one glaring omission.

During the firm's quarterly all-hands meeting, her manager congratulated the entire group on the project's success—but failed to recognize Natalie's leadership or the personal sacrifices she made to ensure it.

Here are the facts—not perception, not ego, but an unshakable reality and testament to Natalie's leadership. While the rest of the team put in their daily nine to five, Natalie was regularly putting in eight-to-midnights (plus many weekends). She was the one solving problems no one else even knew existed, absorbing the pressure so others didn't have to, and ensuring the entire project didn't just get done but got done flawlessly. She wasn't asking for special treatment. She wasn't acting bigger than the team. But the truth is—what she gave up, what she sacrificed—*was greater* than anyone else.

Her manager knew it. He was fully aware of the effort, the late nights, the personal cost. That's exactly why her recognition *had* to reflect it. It needed to match the weight of what she gave.

Leadership comes with responsibility—and when that responsibility leads to success, it deserves to be seen and singled out. This is where Maslow's hierarchy of needs offers valuable insight. Esteem—the need for respect, recognition, and a sense of accomplishment—is a critical layer of human motivation. For Natalie, this need went underserved.

While the team's recognition addressed her desire for belonging and shared success, the absence of specific acknowledgment for her leadership left her personal esteem needs unmet. She felt unnoticed, despite knowing that her work was pivotal. This lack of validation created internal conflict for her: she didn't want to advocate for herself and appear self-serving, yet the omission of individual recognition stung Natalie deeply.

Natalie's experience underscores why esteem is essential, particularly in professional growth. As individuals take on new challenges and roles, acknowledgment of their contributions can fuel their confidence, affirm their value, and motivate them to continue excelling. For leaders, it's a reminder that recognition must go beyond the collective to honor individual contributions, especially when someone is stepping into a new and demanding role.

A great leader would approach Natalie's situation differently. Here's how MADE's principles and a great leader might have addressed Natalie's esteem needs:

- Public Recognition for Contribution: A solid leader wouldn't stop at generic praise. They'd publicly and personally acknowledge Natalie's unique role, highlighting the skills and resilience she demonstrated throughout the project. This recognition would affirm her competence and her sacrifice and cause her to feel greatly valued.
- Opportunities for Growth: Esteem isn't just about a pat on the back. A solid leader might invite Natalie to share her insights with other teams or mentor junior project managers. This would reinforce her

importance with new eyes and attention, and grow the respect others have for her, all while giving her new opportunities to shine. (This also inspires others that may see Natalie's success as inspiration.)

- Regular Feedback and Support: A solid leader wouldn't wait for an annual review. They'd provide prompt and consistent feedback, ensuring Natalie feels supported and knows her work is appreciated in real time.

By addressing Natalie's esteem needs, the leader creates an environment where she feels empowered and inspired to tackle even greater challenges. She becomes not just an effective team member but an inspired one, driven by both recognition and purpose.

A MADE Leader's Commitment to Esteem

Remember, for MADE leaders, esteem isn't a box to check; it's a fundamental aspect of creating sustainable motivation. (The key word here is *sustainable.*) Esteem ensures that individuals move beyond the *deficiency mindset* into one of growth and aspiration.

When leaders nurture esteem, they cultivate a culture of continuous improvement, loyalty, and achievement. By embracing growth motivators and fostering a sense of esteem, great leaders unlock the potential in themselves and their teams—it's about elevating people, ensuring they feel seen, valued, and ready to contribute to something greater than themselves.

Natalie's pivotal role in her project and Haley Ward's journey are powerful reminders that when individuals are supported in their pursuit of recognition and self-respect, they don't just *survive*—they *thrive*. And when they thrive, the organization rises with them.

MADE Leadership Action

- Implement a weekly shout-out for team achievements. Small acknowledgments like "You did great with making that presentation both logical and inspirational!" go a long way in building esteem.
- Highlight individual effort. Publicly acknowledging an individual's specific skills or talents meets the esteem need by highlighting their competence and reinforcing their sense of accomplishment. This builds both self-respect and respect from peers.
- Identify tangible impacts. Helping employees see how their work makes a difference satisfies their desire for achievement and recognition. It builds their internal sense of pride and reinforces their value to the organization, fulfilling both their intrinsic and extrinsic esteem needs.

5. Self-Actualization

The peak of Maslow's hierarchy—self-actualization—is often romanticized yet rarely understood. This is the stage where individuals realize their full potential, not just as professionals but as human beings. It's about living authentically, working with purpose, and embodying what Maslow himself described as, "What one can be, one must be."

I like to define it as the ability to boldly declare, "I am exactly where I am supposed to be in life," knowing that every effort and decision you've made (even the bad ones) has led you to this moment—to the right position, serving the right audience, with the right and unique gift God has given you.

Maslow believed self-actualization was rare—maybe one percent of people ever reached it. But newer research suggests the number is likely much higher. You can't fault him for the estimate. Self-actualization isn't an exact science—it's more of an art. Even today, psychologists struggle to define it clearly, let alone measure it. But what we do know is this: reaching that level requires brutal honesty, real self-awareness, and the courage to step outside your comfort zone. There's no checklist. No shortcut. Just a deep, personal commitment to becoming the version of yourself you were actually built to be.

Most leaders stop short.

They manage paychecks (basic needs), provide job security (safety), maybe host a few team lunches or holiday parties (belonging). Some go a little further and hand out praise or promotions to check the esteem box. But very few lead from the top of the ladder.

Self-actualized leadership isn't easy, and self-actualized leaders don't just manage people. They mobilize them. They don't chase culture—they build it. And they don't just keep the ship afloat—they give people a reason to sail. That's the kind of leadership some of us watched emerge in a quiet corner of northern Maine, where a new generation wasn't just trained to lead, but called to it.

Case Study: Banking on a Bigger Why

Northern Maine doesn't move fast—but it moves with meaning. In Aroostook County, people remember your name, your work, and whether you meant what you said. That's the soil where Acadia Federal Credit Union grew its roots—deep, steady, and built on trust.

For years, Acadia thrived under the leadership of Dave Desjardins, a sharp, disciplined CEO who knew how to grow smart. He understood the business, protected the margins, and kept the institution financially healthy. He was the kind of leader who made sure the lights stayed on and the numbers lined up perfectly *every time*. His legacy is one of strength and stewardship. I've met the man . . . he's a great one for sure.

But every great leader eventually hands off the baton—and waiting in the wings was Joey Cannan, the Executive Vice President, poised to be next in line.

Joey wasn't just another numbers guy—he had vision. Not just for sharper operations, but for something bigger. He believed that Acadia could be more than a financial institution. It could be a force for good—a true community enhancer. Not just a place that managed accounts, but one that helped build better lives in the very towns where Joey himself was born and raised.

Still, like many rising leaders, Joey found himself pulled in multiple directions. Meeting expectations. Honoring legacy. Avoiding disruption. So much to do, so many plates to keep spinning.

That's when we sat down.

As his newly hired executive coach, I didn't bring a spreadsheet to our first coaching session. I brought a question. Just one.

"When it's all said and done," I asked, "what do you want your legacy at Acadia to be?"

It hit him hard. Not because he hadn't thought about it—but because no one had ever asked him *that* early. Before the title. Before the corner office. Before the ink on the CEO nameplate even dried.

Joey paused. That kind of question forces you to look past the job description and straight into the mirror. Then Joey opened up. He talked about his love for the region, his dream of serving underserved populations, and the possibility of rethinking how a credit union could partner with local schools, nonprofits, and small businesses—not just through lending, but through leadership, education, and empowerment.

What Joey needed wasn't just opportunity. He needed alignment and the space to connect *what he would do* with *why it should matter.* And that's what self-actualization's all about: not just climbing the ladder but knowing *why* you're climbing it. And who benefits when you get to the top.

Inspiring leaders like Joey don't wait for permission to lead with purpose. They find their *why,* then build the systems to support it.

Together, we leveraged the MADE framework to help Joey clarify his values, communicate his vision with confidence, and map out tangible ways Acadia could evolve into not just a stronger bank but a louder voice for the people of Aroostook County.

Joey's ideas sparked new conversations. His authenticity energized his team. And his leadership became an example of what's possible when *strategy* meets *self-awareness*.

And Dave? He saw the shift. He respected it. He recognized in Joey not just continuity—but evolution. A new chapter built on the same foundation—just written with deeper ink.

If you want a team that thrives, you don't start with tactics. You start with truth. And that truth starts in the heart of a leader. It's the space where vision and execution meet. Where leadership stops being a role and starts becoming a calling.

Joey Cannan found that space.

I won't steal his thunder by sharing the ideas he's working on—those are his stories to tell. But I'll say this: I've seen the depth of his thinking, and I've seen the heart behind it. And I have full confidence in the impact he's going to make.

His story isn't finished—not even close. Much like yours, it's just starting, in fact. And I can't wait to see all the good Joey brings to Acadia Federal and the communities it serves.

That's the power of realizing self-actualization.

That's what purpose looks like in motion.

And in a place like northern Maine, *that's what people remember.*

Leadership in Action: Creating a Culture of Self-Actualization

If, like Joey, you're serious about fostering self-actualization in your workplace, with your team, here's where to start:

Empower Passion Projects

Create opportunities for employees to work on what lights them up—innovation labs, hackathons, initiatives.

This isn't about *"extra credit"* work; it's about giving people a reason to care. Let them tackle something meaningful and watch their energy skyrocket. *The result?* Fresh ideas for the business and employees who actually feel invested. If you're not giving them space for this, don't be surprised when they disengage—or leave.

Link Purpose to Work

Ask: "What about our work excites you personally?" If they can't answer, that's a red flag.

Chances are, no one's ever asked them this before. That's on you. Help them figure it out—dig into what drives them, what gets them out of bed, and connect it to their role. If their job feels like just a paycheck, you've got a problem. Fix it. Purpose is fuel; without it, the tank's empty.

Foster Autonomy and Trust

Micromanagement kills motivation. Trust them to lead their work, or you'll watch them shut down.

Give people space to do their jobs and make decisions. Check in? Sure, but don't hover. Autonomy says, *"I believe in you."* Micromanagement says, *"I don't trust you."* Guess which one drives performance? Hint: It's not the second one.

Normalize Honest Conversations (Most Important)

Say what needs to be said and expect the same from them. No sugarcoating. No dodging.

"No matter how good you are at it; you still need to get better at giving and receiving feedback." Chances are that if you've ever heard me speak at a keynote or seminar, you've heard this exact line before. I say it with nearly every audience I'm afforded. It's that true and that important.

Feedback isn't a once-a-year box to check—it's your daily job. Be direct, be real, and stop worrying so much about hurting feelings. At the same time, create a space where they can tell you what they want, what's not working, and what's on their mind. Radical candor isn't just a buzzword; it's how you actually get better as a leader and as a team. (Much more on this in the Assessment chapters.)

Case Study: Patagonia – A Blueprint for Purpose-Driven Work

Patagonia didn't just build a brand. They built a movement. What started in 1973 as a few climbers making their own gear has grown into one of the most respected outdoor companies on the planet. Not because they make cool jackets and swaggy hats—but because they live out their values, every single day. (And that's what I respect most.)

Led by CEO Ryan Gellert, Patagonia's leadership doesn't just talk about purpose—they've built it into every job. Employees aren't just selling outdoor gear. They're fighting for clean water, restoring forests, and advocating for environmental justice. Activism isn't a side hustle—it's part of the job description.

And it's not just talk. Through Patagonia's Environmental Internship Program, employees can spend up to two months working for an environmental nonprofit—full-time—and still collect their regular pay and benefits. More than two thousand employees have taken that opportunity, contributing real time and real energy to the causes they care about. It's good for the planet, sure. But more than that? It's *transformative* for the people doing the work.

This is what it looks like when a company actually helps people grow—not just as workers, but as *humans*. That's why Patagonia has a higher than 90 percent retention rate, and why more than 85 percent of their employees say they feel connected to a higher purpose. Compare that to the U.S. average of 30 percent—yikes.

This is what high-level self-actualization at work looks like.

They're not just showing up for a paycheck. They're showing up because the work means something. And when people are connected to work that aligns with who they are, they don't burn out—they light up. They stretch. They grow. They lead.

Now, before you roll your eyes and say, "Yeah, but we're not Patagonia," let me stop you right there. *You don't need a million-dollar internship program to make this real.* You just need the guts to ask your people what drives them—and the willingness to build some space for that into the work.

Here's one of my core mantras—and I stand on this: "It's not about helping your people become better employees. It's about helping your employees become better people."

If you want high-performing, fully engaged, purpose-driven people on your team, then stop managing them like interchangeable parts. Start helping them become the best version of themselves.

Because when people grow, so does everything around them.

MADE Leadership Action

- Provide avenues for personal growth and encourage employees to pursue their passions within the company. This could be a volunteer program, leadership development, or a dedicated project that allows them to contribute in a meaningful way. It doesn't have to be huge; it just has to be authentic and impactful.
- Encourage Personal Development Plans: Support employees in setting and pursuing personal and professional growth goals. This demonstrates a commitment to their development and aligns their aspirations with organizational objectives.
- Facilitate Cross-Departmental Projects: Allow employees to participate in projects outside their usual roles. This exposure broadens their skills and helps them discover new interests, contributing to a more engaged and versatile workforce.
- Implement Regular Feedback Mechanisms: Establish open channels for continuous feedback, enabling employees to express their ideas and feel heard. This practice fosters a culture of trust and collaboration, essential for personal growth.

You Can't Perk Your Way Out and You Can't Climb Blind

Let me tell you about Amy H., a former coaching client. She was a COO at a manufacturing company in central

Massachusetts when I worked with her. My first impression of Amy was high character—sharp, decisive, results-driven.

But her team? Falling apart. High turnover. Low morale. Erratic productivity. Everyone was showing up physically, but emotionally? They were checked out.

Like a lot of leaders, Amy started with surface-level fixes: bonuses, flex time, even piloting a four-day workweek. It bought her a little goodwill—but no real change. People were still disengaged, disconnected, and disillusioned.

That's when we started working together.

I asked her to stop looking at the symptoms and start digging into the root. We used Maslow's hierarchy of needs as a reality check. And what that mirror showed was this: her people were stuck at the base level.

Safety and Security? *Shaky.*

Belonging? *Nonexistent.*

Relationships and Esteem? *Sporadic and superficial.*

They weren't lazy. They were *unseen.*

They weren't unwilling. They were *unheard.*

Amy didn't flinch. She got honest. She owned the fact that after a couple of rounds of poorly communicated layoffs, trust was fractured. That collaboration across teams was minimal. That even her praise—while well-intentioned—lacked personal connection.

After her acknowledgment, something clicked.

Amy realized she'd been managing performance, not *fueling potential.* And if she wanted real change, she had to start meeting people where they actually were—and create space for them to grow from there.

So she did.

She rolled up her sleeves, started hosting open updates to rebuild a sense of safety and stability. She implemented structured 1-on-1s to re-establish belonging and connection. And she didn't just hand out assignments—she helped her team find projects that aligned with their own personal growth goals. She made as much room as one could in manufacturing for self-direction, creativity, and contribution—the exact ingredients needed for people to step into *self-actualization*.

Turnover dropped—*slightly*. Productivity climbed—*slightly*. But more importantly, the people changed—*greatly*.

It's a tough industry, so I won't sit here and tell you everything was peachy keen after the changes Amy made. But I can tell you more employees started showing up like *owners* instead of *renters*. I just wish we'd started the work sooner. Things were trending in the right direction, but not fast enough to outrun the deeper organizational changes that eventually hit Amy and her team. It felt to me like being down twenty in the fourth quarter—cutting the deficit in two—then watching the clock run out.)

Amy doesn't work at that company anymore. But I honestly believe she left it better than she found it. Not just more productive—but more *human*. That's what real leadership is about. And that's what self-actualization looks like at work.

I haven't seen Amy in years, but my good friend Preston recently told me she's now leading operations at a manufacturing plant in central Maine—and she's killing it. No surprise there. Cheers, Amy!

Real leaders don't waste their time slapping Band-Aids on deep organizational wounds. (A lesson Amy learned, which was the key reason for her departure.) They don't mistake shallow perks—pizza parties, meaningless titles, or one-time bonuses—for true motivation. They understand that real engagement, the kind that fuels long-term success, only happens when people's fundamental needs are met. And it takes time.

When employees are anxious about job security, drowning in unrealistic workloads, or left out of critical communication, no amount of surface-level incentives will change their motivation. You can't perk your way out of a broken culture.

Teams thrive when they feel safe, respected, and connected to their work. Leaders who truly get this don't chase gimmicks; they prioritize the essentials—clarity, trust, and a workplace where people can breathe, contribute, and grow.

That said, let's be clear: No one can truly motivate someone else.

Too many leaders carry the unnecessary burden of trying to motivate their people. But motivation isn't something you can hand out—it's something each person has to ignite within themselves.

At the end of the day, I repeat, *all motivation is self-motivation.*

MADE leaders must understand that motivation is deeply personal and must be self-driven. By embracing the four pillars of MADE, leaders create environments where motivation flows freely, guiding their teams toward growth and fulfillment.

At the heart of this journey is Maslow's hierarchy—a blueprint for understanding what drives us as human beings. Many leaders use this framework to address foundational needs like safety and belonging, laying the groundwork for connection and collaboration. But the pinnacle of leadership, self-actualization, is where the magic truly happens. It's the moment when effort blooms into purpose, where individuals don't just meet expectations—they redefine them. Self-actualization turns work into legacy, and leaders into change makers.

Motivation doesn't stop at inspiration—it must be anchored in action. The best leaders build cultures where safety leads to stability, belonging fosters connection, and esteem fuels the hunger to grow. They don't just climb mountains; they make sure others are climbing alongside them. Because true leadership isn't measured by individual achievements—it's defined by how many lives you elevate along the way.

We've made it clear—motivation, especially self-motivation, *is everything*. But let's be honest: even the most fired-up, driven leader won't get far without accurate directions.

This is why MADE leaders don't stop at motivation; they demand deep, unfiltered *Assessment*. Because you can't fix what you won't face, and you won't change what you refuse to own. Motivation is the fuel, but assessment is the GPS. Without it, you're just moving in circles, burning energy, mistaking motion for progress.

The next step in the MADE journey?

The kind of honest self-reflection that comes with focused Assessment.

5

Assessment – Facing the Truth, No Matter What

Leadership isn't simply like physical strength—it is strength. It's the backbone, the muscles, and the grit that carries the weight of decisions, people, and progress. And just like your body can't lift without a solid core, your leadership crumbles without the motivation that powers it.

Weak motivation means shaky leadership.

But strong motivation means you're ready to stand tall, carry the load, and push through the toughest challenges.

You wouldn't strut into a gym, load up an Olympic barbell with weight plates, and attempt a heavy lift without first knowing your limits—what your body can handle, where your strengths lie, and where you risk injury.

Leadership is no different. If you think you're ready to carry the heavy load of responsibility, it's time to find out. Can your leadership frame bear the stress when the pressure mounts? Are you steady enough to weather the storms? Or will you crumble when it counts most?

Think of Assessment as your leadership "stress test." It's not just about knowing your strengths; it's about being brutally honest with yourself. Are you showing up as the leader you claim to be? Are there gaps in your frame—weak points you've ignored? This isn't about making a safe little list of pros and cons to file away. Nah. This is about stepping into the arena of radical self-awareness, facing the tough truths, and committing to growing stronger where it counts.

Take a look in the mirror. Look harder than you think you need to. What's the state of your leadership muscles? Have you been skipping leg day—avoiding the hard, unglamorous work that builds real strength? Are your leadership calves steady and ready, or trembling from neglect? Is your back strong enough to lift your team, your goals, and your vision when the weight is on your shoulders, or will you collapse under the heft?

In the next two chapters, let's see what you can really lift—and then let's build the strength to farmer walk that weight across the finish line.

Expanding the Mirror: Why Feedback Is Essential

You can't become your best self and self-actualize without being self-aware. And you can't be fully self-aware without feedback. You'll never see the full picture of yourself alone. You aren't enough mirror to catch all your own mess. That's why feedback isn't optional for true leaders. Your growth demands reflection, and real reflection requires another set of eyes.

I stood on a stage in Terre Haute, Indiana, and made this very point just a few months ago. Normally, in a setup like that, the lights are so bright you can barely see past the first few rows. But that day the lighting tech must've missed a row, because I could see all the way to the back wall. And right in the middle of talking about self-awareness, a thought hit me. I paused, looked out at the crowd, and said:

"I'd guess there are about 400 people in this room right now . . . and I can see every single one of you perfectly. All except for one. Who can't I see?"

They were sharp. It didn't take long for the audience to catch on—

The only person in that room I couldn't see . . . was me.

"And that's why I need feedback!" I shouted.

Then I gave it to them straight—and loud.

"I need somebody to tell me if I've got toilet paper hanging off my shoe."

Then I pointed to a guy sitting near the front row—real moment, real dude—and said, "I need you to tell me, 'Hey bro, zip it up,' if my fly's down."

That one got a laugh, and yeah, I got a little self-conscious, because what if it was?

But I wasn't done.

"I need someone to tap their nose and say, 'Hey, might wanna grab a tissue—you've got a little issue.'"

You can't fix what you don't know. And if nobody has the guts to tell you, you'll keep walking around thinking you look like a legit leader—when really, you're out here looking like Boo-Boo the Fool.

We can't fix what we won't face.

And we can't face what we can't see.

No matter how skilled you think you are at giving or receiving feedback, you still have to get better. Feedback isn't just a tool—it's the foundation of growth. If you want to improve, if you want to develop into the best version of yourself, then you have to make peace with one simple fact: You need other people's perspectives.

And when it comes to self-awareness and assessment, receiving feedback is where the real work happens. That means we have to get real about something most people avoid: the raw, unfiltered importance of honest conversations.

Few books capture the power of difficult conversations better than *Crucial Conversations: Tools for Talking When Stakes Are High* by Joseph Grenny, Kerry Patterson, Ron McMillan, Al Switzler, and Emily Gregory. If you haven't read it, add it to your list immediately. This book is a game-changer for leaders, professionals, and frankly, anyone who wants to improve the way they communicate.

These authors make a profound and often overlooked point: "The mistake most of us make in our crucial conversations is we believe that we have to choose between telling the truth and keeping a friend."

That's exactly where most people get it wrong. Too often, we assume that honesty and relationships are at odds with each other. We either sugarcoat the truth to keep the peace, or we deliver the truth so harshly that it damages relationships beyond repair. But the best leaders—and the most effective teams—understand that honest conversations, handled correctly, don't destroy relationships; they strengthen them.

Too often the internal debate for a leader often sounds like this: "Do I tell the truth and risk losing this person, or do I soften it and keep them on board?" Keeping an underperforming employee comfortable at the expense of the team, the mission, or the company's long-term success isn't leadership—it's avoidance. And it's an all-too-common leadership failure. Nothing erodes morale faster than watching teammates with low standards or poor behavior get rewarded with job security. The best workplaces don't avoid tough conversations; they create environments where truth and trust can coexist.

Friedrich Nietzsche once said, "The strength of a person's spirit would then be measured by how much 'truth' he could tolerate, or more precisely, to what extent he needs to have it diluted, disguised, sweetened, muted, or falsified."

To that end, here's a question for you: How much truth can you handle? How much do you need the real truth about you silenced or sugarcoated?

Your ability to be self-aware, grow as a leader, and maximize your potential is directly tied to your willingness to hear the truth. And if you're not ready for that, no assessment—no matter how well-designed—will help you reach the level of leadership you're capable of.

For organizations, the same principle applies: How much truth can your culture handle?

Growth starts with truth, and truth starts with the courage to receive feedback.

One of the biggest obstacles to growth—both personally and professionally—is our discomfort with honest conversations. We tiptoe around the truth, afraid to offend, but in doing so, we rob people of the opportunity to improve.

In my years as a professor at Husson University, teaching Principles of Management and Organizations in the undergraduate business and MBA program, I drilled two words into my students: Effectiveness and Efficiency.

- **Effectiveness:** Getting the job done. A task is either done or undone, and a manager's job is to ensure things get done.
- **Efficiency:** Getting the job done with fewer resources—less time, less effort, fewer people, less waste.

How can a manager make their team, department, or organization effective and efficient without honest conversations?

How do you improve processes without identifying and communicating flaws?

How do you help employees grow if you never tell them where they're falling short?

It can't be done. It's impossible. No one gets better without proper assessment, and proper assessment always includes feedback from others.

The Hardest Truth: Real Self-Awareness

Great leaders always choose truth.

Not convenient truth. Not curated truth. The full, unfiltered, sometimes uncomfortable truth. Because without truth, real self-awareness is impossible. And that's where most people go wrong.

They reinforce their own narratives, replay past experiences through a biased lens, and call it reflection. Self-awareness isn't just about *knowing yourself* but about understanding *how others experience you*. Most people think they're self-aware, but what they're really doing is just running an internal monologue of who *they believe they are.*

Real self-awareness forces you to confront the gaps between three perspectives:

1. *Who you think you are.*
2. *Who you actually are.*
3. *How others experience you.*

That confrontation is uncomfortable, which is why most people avoid it.

When self-awareness is done wrong, it leads to self-doubt, insecurity, and frustration. It can damage confidence instead of building it.

And statistically speaking, most people are doing it wrong.

Psychologist and leadership expert Tasha Eurich, in her book *Insight*, conducted groundbreaking research on self-awareness. Her findings: 95 percent of people believe they are self-aware, but in reality, only 10 percent—or even as low as 5 percent—actually are.

That means the vast majority of us are operating under a dangerous illusion.

But life will correct you.

Those willing to face the truth head-on find that self-awareness becomes the key to growth, strong leadership, and resilience. And the best way to start? Understanding the Three Selves Theory—a framework that reveals why self-awareness is so difficult, and why mastering it separates good leaders from great ones.

The Three Selves: Reckon with the Gap

Gabriel García Márquez once said, "Everyone has three lives: a public life, a private life, and a secret life." That's not just poetic—it's the truth.

Everyone—you, me, the most powerful leaders, and the most private individuals—operates within these three layers of self. Each plays a role in how we move through the world, how others perceive us, and ultimately, how successful we are in navigating relationships, leadership, and personal growth.

But here's what most people miss: self-awareness isn't just about knowing yourself—it's about knowing how the world experiences you.

Because no matter what story you tell yourself, *life gets the last word*. It won't say it gently. It communicates the message through *lost opportunities, failed connections, and painful lessons* if your self-perception and reality don't align.

And this is exactly why I introduced the ABCD Cycle of Success in Chapter 1.

That framework—the continuous cycle of Attention, Belief, Chance, and Delivery—reveals whether you are truly in sync with how others perceive you. Every time you move through that cycle, you are forced to *reckon with the gap* between who you think you are and how others actually experience you. If that gap is too wide, life will let you know—not with whispers, but with setbacks that make you wonder why nothing seems to be working.

And if you really want to understand where that disconnect exists, you have to start with Márquez's Three Selves.

The Public Self: The Image You Project

Your public self is the version of you that the world sees. It's the polished, curated, edited version that shows up in meetings, on social media, in interviews, and at networking events. It's the job title, the reputation, the carefully crafted and controlled first impression you try to make.

For some, the public self is fairly aligned with who they really are. For others, it's a complete performance.

Think about the person who seems confident, well-spoken, and completely in control at work. That's their public self. But what if, behind closed doors, they are crippled by self-doubt, questioning every decision, fearing they aren't enough? That's where the disconnect begins.

Your public self isn't necessarily dishonest. It serves a purpose. It allows you to function professionally, build credibility, and navigate social expectations. But the danger comes when the public self becomes more about perception than reality. When it's more about keeping up an image than actually being that person.

And if your public self outpaces your ability to actually deliver, the ABCD Model will correct you in due time.

You might get attention, but belief in you will fade if you can't back it up. You might get a chance, but if you can't deliver, you won't get another one. And if that happens enough, your public self collapses under its own weight.

The Private Self: The Real You Behind Closed Doors

Your private self is who you are when the cameras are off—when the performance isn't necessary. It's the version of you that your closest friends, family, and inner circle know.

This is the version of you that doesn't have to be "on" all the time.

For some people, their public self and private self are nearly identical. What you see is what you get. For others, the difference is staggering. Think about the leader who commands a room at work but feels completely lost at home. Think about the influencer who seems perfectly put together on Instagram, but, behind the scenes, their life is unraveling. *(It's a ton of those!)*

If your private self and public self are completely different, it creates strain, exhaustion, and burnout. You begin to feel like you're living two lives, constantly switching between personas. And when that happens, you stop feeling *seen*. Because no one actually knows you. They only know *versions of you*.

If your private self is weak—if you don't do the work to build real substance behind your image—you will break. Because life doesn't reward performances. It rewards who you actually are.

This is where the *belief* phase of the ABCD Model comes into play. You might be able to get *attention* with a strong public self, but to build real *belief*—to have people trust you, follow you, and invest in you—you need something *real* beneath the surface.

And that's where your *secret self* comes in.

The Secret Self: The Buried Truths

Your secret self is the part of you that no one—not your best friend, not your spouse, not even your therapist (unless you're brutally honest)—gets full access to.

This is where your deepest fears, regrets, ambitions, and insecurities live.

Some people keep their secret self well-managed, using it as a place for reflection and growth. Others bury things here so deeply that it slowly crushes them.

This is the part of you that holds the things you've never admitted out loud.

The thing you did in college that still fills you with shame—the one you'd be horrified if anyone ever found out about.

The jealousy you feel toward a close friend's success, even though you'd never say it aloud.

The resentment you carry toward someone you love—someone you're supposed to forgive, but deep down, you haven't.

The fear that you're not actually as good as people think you are—that one day, they'll figure it out, and it will all fall apart. (Imposter Syndrome)

If your secret self is filled with unresolved pain, guilt, or insecurity, it will leak into everything else. It will shape your private self, which will inevitably shape your public self.

Straight up: what you refuse to deal with in your secret self will eventually deal with you. It will manifest as self-sabotage, as emotional walls, as unhealthy coping mechanisms. And when that happens, the ABCD cycle and life will hold you accountable.

Because if you don't face your secret self, you will hit a wall in the chance and delivery stages. Life will only let you fake it for so long before it demands the real thing. And without the real thing the opportunities dry up.

When the Selves Don't Sync

As we discussed in Chapter One, the ABCD Model is a continuous cycle. You get *attention*, you build *belief*, you earn a *chance*, and then you must *deliver.* Each time you cycle through, you move higher—but only if you've done the work to keep up.

And that's why understanding the three selves is so important. Because if your public self is built on illusion, if your private self is disconnected, and if your secret self is full of unresolved baggage, life will expose it.

At some point, the way you see yourself and the way the world sees you have to match. Otherwise, the cycle stops. You lose credibility, you lose momentum, and eventually, you lose confidence.

So the real question is—*are you brave enough to look at all three selves and do the work to make sure they align?* Because that's what real success, real leadership, and real fulfillment are built on.

The Other Side of the Coin: Receiving Feedback Without Losing Your Mind

Giving feedback is one thing. Receiving it? That's a whole different beast. But sometimes it takes words from other people to let us know if our secret, private, and public lives are out of sync. We need to know what other people can *see* about us. Is more of our private life visible than we thought? Or worse . . . are our secrets out?

Most of us like to believe we're open to feedback—that we can take it constructively and grow from it. But the truth is, criticism stings. It doesn't matter how well-intentioned it is; there's a natural, human instinct to get defensive, justify ourselves, or even flip the script and critique the person critiquing us.

But we don't get better without feedback. And if you want to be an effective leader, a high performer, or simply a better version of yourself, you have to get better at receiving it.

What makes it an even tougher pill to swallow is that not everyone is skilled at delivering feedback in a palatable way. Yes, some people are blunt. Some are insensitive and lack emotional intelligence. Some come across harsher than they mean to. Sometimes feedback comes with an agenda. Remember my DEIB consultation horror story from last chapter? But if you shut down every time feedback isn't perfectly packaged, you will miss out on valuable insight that could help you grow.

So, before you dismiss feedback because you didn't like the tone or the delivery—pause. Force yourself to answer the following questions:

Is there any truth in this, even if I don't like how it was said?

Am I reacting to the content or the delivery?

If I take my emotions out of it, is this something I can use to improve?

How we *receive* feedback is just as important as how we *give* it. If receiving feedback is a struggle, consider it an area for growth—a muscle that needs to be strengthened, not ignored. And this is exactly why *Assessment* is one of the foundational principles in the MADE framework.

A Few Tips to Get Better at Receiving Feedback

- Separate the message from the messenger. Not everyone will give feedback the "right" way. That doesn't mean the feedback itself is wrong. Eat the meat and spit out the bones.
- Resist the urge to fire back. It's tempting to criticize the person giving you feedback, especially if they weren't tactful. Don't let your ego hijack the opportunity to improve.
- Assume positive intent (until proven otherwise). Most feedback isn't meant to tear you down—it's meant to help you grow. Even if it's not delivered perfectly, assume it comes from a place of honesty rather than hostility.
- Reflect before you react. Your first reaction to feedback is usually emotional. Give it time. Sit with it. Get

curious before you get furious. Think critically before deciding if it's valid or not.

- Recognize feedback as a tool, not a threat. Great leaders, great professionals, and great human beings seek out feedback. If no one ever gives you honest criticism, it's probably not because you're perfect—it's because they don't think you can handle it. And that's a bigger problem.

Know Your Gauges: Why Assessment is a Leadership Survival Skill

Motivation unlocks the door, but assessment charts the course.

Imagine arriving in a foreign city with no map or GPS. What happens? You inevitably get lost. The same is true for leadership without self-assessment. A thorough assessment is your map, your GPS, guiding you toward actionable success and preventing aimless wandering through challenges.

My first car was a 1979 Chevrolet Caprice Classic—Carolina blue all over, except for one darker blue quarter panel and a matching dark blue bonnet swapped in to replace the rusted-out originals. By the time I got it, the car was already more than twenty years old and well past its prime. But I loved that car—not because it was reliable or even remotely close to perfect, but because it was mine. That was about the only thing it had going for it, because almost everything on it was *broken.*

The windshield wipers worked—until they got wet. So, if it rained too hard, I had to pull over.

The heat worked—but only in the summer. If it was hot, I was hotter.

The air conditioning would kick in—but only when it was cold outside. So, if the temps sank too low, I just stayed home.

But the worst of all? The gas gauge was broken.

That doesn't seem like a big deal—until you actually have to drive a car like that. I never knew when I was about to run out of gas. *I had to guess.* And guessing wrong? That meant long walks to the closest service station with my too-frequent sidekick—Uncle Willie's old gas can.

I called it *Carl*—because my car kept taking L's.

Car + L = Carl.

Every time Carl and I hung out, it cost me.

Wasted time. Endless frustration. And the constant stress of not knowing whether I'd make it to where I was going.

Worst of all, I worked some nights until 10 PM—getting out oftentimes after some gas stations had already closed. Running out of gas wasn't just an inconvenience; it was a real problem. This was 1993, before most people had cell phones. So, no quick call to my parents or a friend. If I ran out of gas, I was on my own. I'd had that experience enough to know that I didn't want to have it again.

So, to avoid getting stranded, I had no choice but to constantly stop for gas, whether I needed it or not. I might have had a half-tank, a quarter-tank, or just fumes—sometimes I never knew until it was too late. Sometimes I spent my last five bucks, my lunch money, buying gas I wasn't sure I even needed. The not-knowing hurt, and the guessing game was costly and infuriating. Here's the thing: a lot of people lead just like that, always guessing.

They don't understand that assessment isn't just a leadership tool—it's a survival skill. Think of it like your car's dashboard.

I drove that car without working gauges for years, and let me tell you, it taught me just how valuable a functioning instrument panel is. You don't realize how much you rely on the information those gauges provide until you don't have it. And once you don't? You never take those gauges for granted again.

Now, imagine having a fully functional dashboard—one that clearly shows your fuel level, speed, engine health, and tire pressure—but choosing to completely ignore it. You never check the gas gauge, you disregard the engine light, and you roll past every warning sign. Then, one day, you run out of gas.

Is that the car's fault? No. That's *on you*!

Leadership works the same way. You can have all the tools, all the signs, all the indicators telling you where you stand and what needs attention—but if you choose to ignore them, the speeding tickets (from ignoring the speedometer), the overheating (from ignoring the temp), the breakdown (from ignoring the check engine light that's been on for three months) . . . that's all *on you.*

That's why Assessment matters. Neglect leads to delays, breakdowns, and failures. A great leader doesn't gamble their journey on luck or ignorance. They check the dashboard, adjust as needed, and keep the engine running. Leaders who skip regular self-assessments are driving blind. They risk burnout, blind spots, fractured relationships, and blown opportunities.

The MADE Leadership Assessment is a solid dashboard for leaders. It helps you see where you stand, where you're running low, and what needs immediate attention.

Because *guessing* is not a strategy. *Knowing* is.

A complete assessment of a leader should include these three Cs, all critical areas:

- **Core Competencies:** Do they have the technical ability needed for the role? Are they good at the work?
- **Cultural Alignment:** Does the leader embody the organization's values? Are they a personality fit?
- **Character Skills:** Is the leader Motivated? Does the leader possess Integrity?

Each of the three Cs is essential for true leadership success. Ignoring any one of them is like taking that road trip with a missing gauge. You won't get far without risking a breakdown. Regular assessments of all three areas help leaders stay balanced, effective, and ready to lead their teams. But make no mistake, of the three Cs, character skills are the only non-negotiables.

I often say, "Hire and promote for character. You can teach the rest." Without character skills, technical ability and cultural fit crumble under pressure. A leader without integrity, motivation, or self-awareness isn't a leader—*they're a liability*. Character defines whether someone will rise to the challenge, hold themselves accountable, and earn the respect of their team.

The MADE system cuts through the noise and gets straight to the heart of what matters: assessing and developing leaders who don't just show up but *show up right.* It's not about checking boxes; it's about building leaders who have the guts to lead with purpose, act with integrity, and inspire real change. MADE doesn't coddle—it equips you with the tools to face the hard truths and do the work. Because without character, leadership is nothing more than a hollow title.

Case Study: A Leader's Assessment-Driven Change

In a coaching session with an aspiring leader, Rian, we reviewed his assessment results together.

When the feedback showed empathy and active listening as growth areas, Rian could have made excuses. But he didn't. Instead, he took a breath, embraced the data, and made a commitment to improve.

Over the next few months, he changed the way he engaged with his team—leaning into intentional listening, asking questions to understand rather than to respond, and ensuring his actions reflected genuine care.

The results were transformative. His team began to trust him in ways they hadn't before, speaking up more openly and collaborating more effectively. Productivity didn't just increase—it soared because Rian's willingness to face the truth about his leadership gaps created a ripple effect of trust and accountability across his team.

This is the power of assessment: it doesn't just point out weaknesses; it gives you a roadmap to become the leader your team needs. Rian's story isn't an anomaly; it's proof that honest self-assessment, paired with intentional action, doesn't tweak leadership—it reinvents it.

Now it's your turn. But before you dive into the MADE Leader Assessment, I'm asking you to do exactly what I asked Rian to do: Take five to ten minutes to ground yourself in self-awareness. Reflection is the prerequisite for transformation. So, start with this question—a foundational one worth revisiting quarterly—and write down your honest thoughts in the space below. Be blunt, be real, and let this exercise uncover where you are as a leader today so you can chart a clearer path to where you want to be tomorrow.

What habits or behaviors am I tolerating in myself that don't align with my values? Write them down here or on a separate sheet.

The MADE Leadership Lens: A Guide to the Self-Assessment

Now that you're fired up and ready to tackle this, let's zero in on the leadership characteristics that truly matter. These are the gauges every leader must keep in check to ensure they're steering their team—and themselves—the MADE way.

Let's dive in!

The characteristics associated with a MADE Leader include the following:

1. Self-motivation
2. Emotional intelligence
3. Self-awareness
4. Accountability
5. Growth mindset
6. Adaptability
7. Integrity
8. Assertiveness
9. Consistency
10. Effective communication
11. Relationship management
12. Resilience
13. Inclusion and belonging advocacy
14. Conflict resolution skills
15. Prioritization of self-care
16. Balance between empathy and productivity
17. Transparency
18. Respect for boundaries
19. Patience and tolerance
20. Commitment to continuous learning and development

These characteristics emphasize the foundation of leadership qualities that are universally important, yet they are highly adaptable to individual industries, roles, and organizations. They are not meant to be rigid definitions but instead a starting point for reflection. Each leader must consider how these traits manifest in their specific context, refining them to meet the needs of their environment. For instance, *adaptability* for a fast-moving tech leader differs vastly from how a risk management executive at a bank might define it. Both leaders need adaptability, but one might focus on thriving amid constant updates and rapid shifts, while the other prioritizes navigating strict policies with a creative yet compliant mindset.

Below is a guide to inspire thought and application, allowing you and your colleagues to connect these characteristics with their unique situations. The final sentence of each quality *(italicized)* distills the trait into a universal insight. It's designed to be relevant across roles and industries, offering a clear takeaway for reflection and action in your unique leadership context.

The 20 MADE Leadership Traits

1. **Self-Motivation**
   All motivation is self-motivation! In fast-paced industries, self-motivation might mean driving toward goals despite uncertainty. For more structured environments, it could involve finding intrinsic satisfaction in refining routines. *Wherever you are, self-motivation is about moving forward without needing constant external pushes.*

2. **Emotional Intelligence**
   For leaders in highly relational fields, emotional intelligence may involve deeply understanding team dynamics. In more transactional settings, it might focus on recognizing and managing your own emotional triggers. *Always consider how emotions impact decisions and interactions.*

3. **Self-Awareness**
   A creative professional might use self-awareness to tap into strengths that foster innovation, while a compliance officer uses it to recognize when their biases could skew judgment. *Either way, knowing yourself is foundational to growth and leadership.*

4. **Accountability**
   In high-autonomy roles, accountability might mean owning outcomes without direct oversight. In collaborative spaces, it could involve holding others accountable while maintaining trust. *The key to accountability is ensuring your actions align with your commitments.*

5. **Growth Mindset**
   A startup founder might see every setback as a chance to pivot, while a teacher sees it as an opportunity to refine methods for their students. *Growth mindset is about embracing challenges as part of the journey to mastery.*

6. **Adaptability**
   Tech leaders might need adaptability to thrive in rapid innovation cycles, while healthcare workers adapt to

emotional and procedural demands daily. *Adaptability is about staying effective even when circumstances shift unexpectedly.*

7. **Integrity**
   For a salesperson, integrity may mean transparent dealings with clients, while for a nonprofit director, it might mean aligning actions with the organization's mission. *Integrity is non-negotiable—it builds trust in every industry.*

8. **Assertiveness**
   In corporate boardrooms, assertiveness might involve presenting ideas confidently, while for a frontline worker, it could mean advocating for better conditions. *The aim is clear, respectful communication of needs and boundaries.*

9. **Consistency**
   For a project manager, consistency means delivering steady progress, while for a caregiver, it might mean providing predictable emotional support. *Whatever your role, reliability builds trust.*

10. **Effective Communication**
    In customer-facing roles, this might focus on clarity and empathy with clients. For analysts, it could mean presenting data in ways that decision-makers understand. *Tailor your communication approach to make sure your message lands.*

11. **Relationship Management**
    In a sales environment, relationship management might

focus on long-term client loyalty, while for team leaders, it means fostering cohesion. *Strong relationships are the foundation of successful collaboration.*

12. **Resilience**
A small business owner may need resilience to recover from financial setbacks, while a creative professional uses it to bounce back from rejection. *It's about staying grounded and persistent through challenges.*

13. **Inclusion and Belonging Advocacy**
For an HR leader, this might mean implementing equitable and merit-based hiring practices, while a team member can foster inclusion by ensuring all voices are heard in meetings. *Adapt your advocacy to the influence you hold.*

14. **Conflict Resolution Skills**
In customer service, this might involve de-escalating tense interactions, while in leadership, it's about aligning differing priorities within a team. *The goal is to navigate conflicts productively without alienating anyone.*

15. **Prioritization of Self-Care**
In high-pressure jobs, self-care might involve setting work-life boundaries, while in service-oriented fields, it could mean finding ways to recharge emotionally. *Taking care of yourself enables sustained performance.*

16. **Balance Between Empathy and Productivity**
For a manager, this might involve showing

understanding for personal challenges while ensuring deadlines are met. For educators, it's supporting students emotionally while fostering accountability. *Balance is key to effectiveness.*

17. **Transparency**
In leadership, transparency might mean openly sharing the reasoning behind decisions, while in team settings, it's about honesty in feedback. *Transparency builds trust and minimizes misunderstandings.*

18. **Respect for Boundaries**
In remote work, this could involve honoring time zones and work hours, while in caregiving, it's about recognizing emotional limits. *Clear boundaries foster respect and efficiency.*

19. **Patience and Tolerance**
In a customer-facing role, patience means calmly addressing repetitive questions, while in technical fields, it's tolerating trial-and-error processes. *Patience and tolerance require managing frustration and maintaining focus.*

20. **Commitment to Continuous Learning and Development**
For engineers, this might mean keeping up with the latest technologies, while for social workers, it's learning new ways to support clients. *Growth is a constant, regardless of industry.*

These twenty traits, when understood and personalized to your unique environment, become the driving force behind teams that thrive, organizations that innovate, and individuals who lead with purpose. The question isn't whether you can develop these qualities—it's whether you're ready to commit to the work that greatness demands. If you are, the time to start is now, and the best next step you can take is completing the MADE Leadership Aptitude Assessment later in this chapter.

But before we get there, let me first explain how the 20 MADE Leadership Traits have been grouped and distilled into the 8 refined categories presented in the assessment scoring and report.

If you're not into the nitty-gritty, that's okay. Feel free to skip ahead to the next section. But if you're like me and love understanding how things work under the hood, keep reading.

Refining the 20 MADE Leadership Traits into 8 Scorable Categories

The MADE Leadership framework started with 20 distinct traits. To streamline the process and make it more actionable, those traits were distilled into 8 overarching categories. These categories capture the essence of what it takes to drive personal and professional growth, while keeping the evaluation focused and practical.

Category	Traits	Focus
Motivation	Self-Motivation, Resilience, Consistency	*Demonstrates drive, perseverance, and a steady commitment to achieving goals.*
Emotional Intelligence	Emotional Intelligence, Balance Between Empathy and Productivity, Inclusivity and Belonging Advocacy	*Balances personal and team emotions effectively, fostering inclusion and maintaining productivity.*
Self-Awareness	Self-Awareness, Commitment to Continuous Learning and Development, Prioritization of Self-Care	*Reflects on personal actions and growth while maintaining balance and well-being.*
Accountability	Accountability, Integrity, Transparency	*Embraces responsibility, demonstrates ethical behavior, and communicates openly.*
Growth Mindset	Growth Mindset, Adaptability, Patience and Tolerance	*Views challenges as opportunities, adapts effectively, and approaches situations with understanding.*
Adaptability	Adaptability, Resilience, Respect for Boundaries	*Adjusts to changing circumstances while maintaining personal resilience and respecting others.*
Integrity	Integrity, Transparency, Assertiveness	*Acts with honesty and consistency while standing firm on values.*
Communication	Effective Communication, Conflict Resolution Skills, Relationship Management	*Builds strong relationships through clear communication and effective conflict management.*

Guidelines for Taking the MADE Leadership Aptitude Assessment: Self-Assessment

The assessment phase evaluates leaders on the key MADE leadership qualities. To ensure the results are meaningful, it's crucial to approach this process with focus, honesty, and a commitment to self-reflection.

1. Allocate Time Wisely: Set aside ten to fifteen minutes in a quiet, distraction-free space to focus fully on the task.
2. Be Honest and Accurate: Answer truthfully based on your real behaviors and experiences. Growth and insight depend on authenticity.
3. Reflect on Recent Experiences: Use examples from only the last six to twelve months that reflect your leadership style or actions.
4. Focus on Personal Leadership: Keep the focus on your own actions and decisions—not external factors like *your team's performance* or *circumstances beyond your control.* This is about gaining clarity on your individual growth.
5. Understand the Scale: Each question uses a Likert scale (1–5), where:
    - 1 = Never True
    - 2 = Rarely True
    - 3 = Sometimes True
    - 4 = Often True
    - 5 = Always True
6. Consider each statement carefully before selecting your response.

7. Trust Your Gut: Avoid overthinking. Your first instinct is often the most accurate reflection of reality.
8. Approach with Intention: Treat this as an investment in your growth. The effort you put in will directly shape the quality of insights you gain.

These guidelines aim to ensure a meaningful and constructive self-assessment experience. By following them, you'll set yourself up for clear, actionable insights into your leadership development.

Okay. Take a breath.

This is the moment where growth truly begins. The MADE Leadership Aptitude Assessment isn't just a step; it's *The Step*.

The one that sets everything else in motion. Without it, you're navigating this journey without a map, without a GPS, without a dashboard instrument panel—and that's just driving blind. Disaster awaits!

This is your chance to gain clarity, uncover blind spots, and focus your energy where it matters most. Don't cheat yourself out of the insights waiting for you. Visit **TheMADELeader.com** now, complete the assessment, and come back ready to dive deeper into unlocking your leadership potential.

We'll pick up right here in the next chapter. Trust me . . . you'll be ready for what's next!

6

Assessment – The MADE Leader

Taking the MADE Leadership Assessment wasn't just a step—it was a *power move*. Most people dodge the hard truth. You faced it head-on and got clear about where you stand. Think about it: what's the point of a map if you don't know your starting point? The first thing any GPS does is lock in your current location before plotting the path to your destination. That's exactly what you just did.

Now, before you set your sights on that perfect 40 score—the ultimate MADE Leader status—own this moment. Understanding where you are isn't just necessary; it's the foundation of everything that comes next. This isn't about nitpicking gaps. It's about locking in on your strengths and using them to springboard into game-changing growth.

What Your Results Mean

There are two types of scores that we'll focus on and that you can best use as feedback to grow your leadership legs: your MADE Category Scores and your Total MADE Leader Score.

MADE Category Scores

Remember, the MADE Leadership framework started with twenty distinct traits—each a cornerstone of effective leadership. To streamline the process and make it more actionable, those traits were distilled into 8 overarching categories:

1. Motivation
2. Emotional Intelligence
3. Self-Awareness
4. Accountability
5. Growth Mindset
6. Adaptability
7. Integrity
8. Communication

Each category score provides a clear picture of where you excel, where you show potential, and where focused effort could lead to transformative growth.

In this chapter, we'll break down what these scores mean and how to use them to chart your leadership journey. We'll also look at a case study example to get a clearer picture of what the process can look like.

Your scores in the eight leadership categories provide a detailed snapshot of your leadership profile. Each category score ranges from 0 to 5 and corresponds to one of four performance levels, giving you a clear understanding of where you excel and where there's room to grow.

Exceptional Performance ***(Scores from 5.0-4.5)***
You're excelling here. Consider these your leadership superpowers—strengths that you can lean into and build upon. *Example*: A high score in Communication suggests that you're skilled at expressing ideas clearly and fostering understanding. Use this strength to inspire your team and align them toward shared goals.

Strong Capability ***(Scores from 4.4–3.5)***
These scores indicate a solid foundation. With consistent effort, these areas could evolve into standout strengths. *Example*: A strong score in Accountability shows that you reliably follow through on commitments. To refine further, focus on fostering accountability within your team as well.

Show Potential ***(Scores from 3.4–2.5)***
Scores in this range point to untapped opportunities. With intentional focus, these areas can become powerful assets. *Example*: If Adaptability falls here, work on responding to change with positivity and agility to better navigate challenges.

Significant Growth Needed ***(Scores Below 2.5)***
These scores highlight areas where you may be falling short. If leadership has been a struggle, this could be the reason why. Focused growth in these areas could drive significant improvement, transforming your leadership influence, insight, and effectiveness. *Example*: If Integrity falls in this range, prioritize aligning your actions with your stated values to build trust and credibility.

The chart below provides an overview of the eight critical leadership categories within the MADE Leadership framework, offering a summary for individuals who may not yet have taken the MADE Leader Assessment. It outlines key strengths, areas for improvement, and opportunities for focused growth based on potential assessment scores.

MADE Leader Category Breakdown *with* Reflections and Next Steps

Category	**Exceptional Performance** *(5.0–4.5)*	**Strong Capability** *(4.4–3.5)*	**Shows Potential** *(3.4–2.5)*	**Significant Growth Needed** *(Below 2.5)*	***Reflection Prompt***	***Next Step***
Motivation	Inspires others with your drive and vision	Stays motivated and align well with goals	Motivation inconsistent—reconnect with their purpose	Struggles to find drive or align with goals—revisit their "why"	*"What energizes you as a leader? When do you feel the most motivated?"*	*Define a personal mission statement to reconnect with your purpose*
Emotional Intelligence	Navigates emotions and relationships with ease	Manages emotions well and build positive dynamics	Awareness is there but inconsistent—practice recognizing emotional cues	Reactive or disconnected from emotions, impacting relationships	*"How do you respond to stressful interactions? What's one way to improve?"*	*Observe how emotions influence team dynamics and adjust where needed*
Self-Awareness	Understands their strengths, weaknesses, and their impact on others	Aware but could sharpen their reflection	Limited awareness—seek feedback to identify blind spots	Lacks understanding of self, leading to missed opportunities	*"How do your emotions or actions affect others? What feedback surprised you recently?"*	*Ask a peer for one honest insight about how you show up as a leader*
Accountability	Follows through consistently and model ownership for others	Takes ownership but could build team accountability	Accountability is situational—focus on consistent follow-through	Struggles to deliver on commitments, leading to team trust issues	*"What's one recent promise you made—did you deliver on it fully?"*	*Keep a checklist of daily commitments and track your follow-through rate*
Growth Mindset	Embraces challenges and inspire others to see them as opportunities	Approaches challenges constructively but could push further	Fixed mindset tendencies—reframe setbacks as learning opportunities	Resists challenges, often seeing them as threats rather than chances to grow	*"When did you last turn a setback into a lesson? What stopped you from learning?"*	*Reflect weekly on one challenge you faced and the growth it offered*
Adaptability	Thrives in change and guide others through transitions smoothly	Handles change well but could refine agility in complex situations	Adapts when necessary but resists major shifts—work on flexibility	Struggles with change, often leading to frustration or stagnation	*"What's your initial reaction to change? How can you make it more positive?"*	*Take one unexpected change this week and respond by proposing a solution*
Integrity	Actions align with values, building trust and credibility	Integrity is strong but could be tested under pressure	Inconsistent alignment with values—focus on modeling ethical behavior	Struggles to align actions with stated values, eroding trust	*"What's one value you could embody more consistently in your actions?"*	*Identify one action today that reinforces your core values to your team*
Communication	Conveys ideas clearly and inspire alignment within teams	Communication is clear but could improve in difficult situations	Inconsistent communication—work on clarity and tone	Struggles to express ideas, leading to misunderstandings	*"When have you struggled to express yourself? What impact did it have on others?"*	*Practice simplifying a message and confirming understanding in your next meeting*

For those seeking deeper insights, the comprehensive report available after completing the assessment at **TheMADELeader.com** delivers personalized analysis and actionable recommendations. This detailed report is specifically designed to help individuals enhance their leadership style and make meaningful progress. While the chart is a useful snapshot, the official report serves as the definitive resource for transformative growth.

Total MADE Leader Score

Your Total MADE Leader Score offers a comprehensive snapshot of your overall leadership effectiveness, providing a single, clear measure of where you currently stand as a leader. This score distills the critical aspects of leadership into one number, making it easy to understand your overall impact and potential.

By offering a big-picture view, the Total Score helps you identify where you are on your leadership journey and shows you how far you can go. It's not just a score—it's a powerful tool to prioritize your growth, track your progress, and guide your path to becoming a truly transformational leader. It's also a straightforward measurement for intra-team or leadership coaching discussions, making it a valuable tool for goal-setting and progress tracking.

Total MADE Leader Score: Ranges, Interpretations, and Feedback

Score Range	Interpretation	Feedback
40.0–36.0	**Exceptional Leader**	You're excelling across most or all categories. Focus on sustaining your performance and mentoring others.
35.9–31.0	**Strong Leader**	You demonstrate solid leadership capabilities. Refine specific traits to achieve greater consistency and impact.
30.9–26.0	**Developing Leader**	You show potential but have room to grow. Prioritize areas where your category scores indicate opportunities for improvement.
25.9 or Below	**Emerging Leader**	Significant growth is needed across multiple areas. Focus on foundational skills and set clear goals for targeted development.

What Your Total MADE Leader Score Tells You

Alignment Across Categories

Your total score reflects the balance (or imbalance) across the eight leadership categories. For instance, strong scores in Motivation, Integrity, and Communication might be counterbalanced by lower scores in Growth Mindset or Adaptability. Reviewing your category scores alongside your total score helps you identify which areas most influence your overall effectiveness.

Your Leadership Profile

If your Total MADE Leader score is in the **Exceptional Leader** range, you are likely to display well-rounded leadership capabilities and inspire confidence in others. Your challenge is to sustain this performance and actively mentor those around you.

As a **Strong Leader**, you're on solid ground, but refining specific skills—especially those where you scored lower—can elevate your impact even further.

A **Developing Leader** score signals clear potential. Focused effort in one or two key areas can have a significant ripple effect, unlocking higher levels of leadership success.

For an **Emerging Leader**, this is your opportunity to build a strong leadership foundation. Growth starts here with intentional focus on fundamental skills. MADE is the perfect system for you as you prepare to embark on your leadership journey!

Deeper Reflection and Actions

To make the most of your Total MADE Leader Score, reflect on the following questions:

- "Do my individual category scores align with my overall score? If not, why?"
- "Which categories contribute most to my current score?"
- "What would moving up one performance level mean for my career and team?"

Strategic Next Steps

Now that you are a motivated leader, equipped with self-assessment data, you want to be thinking strategically about your next moves. Use your Total MADE Leader Score as the foundation for actionable growth, ensuring your efforts are intentional and aligned with your goals.

As Sun Tzu said, "Strategy without tactics is the slowest route to victory. Tactics without strategy is the noise before defeat." Be sure to incorporate these tactical steps into your strategy.

1. **Identify Your Priority Categories**
   Pinpoint the one or two categories where improvement could have the greatest impact. For example, a *Developing Leader* with low scores in Communication and Self-Awareness might focus on those areas first to enhance collaboration and decision-making.

2. **Leverage Your Strengths**
   Recognize the categories where you scored highest

and use those strengths to support growth in weaker areas. For instance, a strong score in *Emotional Intelligence* can help a leader address challenges in *Accountability* by better understanding team dynamics.

3. **Track Your Progress Over Time**
   Your Total MADE Leader Score isn't static—it's a dynamic tool for tracking your leadership growth over time. Retake the assessment periodically (e.g., quarterly or annually) to measure progress and fine-tune your development plan. By continually interacting with the assessment at **TheMADELeader.com**, you can gain clear, actionable insights into where you stand as a leader at any time. There's no reason to stay in the dark when such a simple step can light the way to your next level.

Case Study: Unlocking Leadership Potential in an Aspiring Energy Services Leader

Jake was a team lead at a mid-sized energy services company. He was thirty-eight, ambitious, and eager to grow as a leader.

I met Jake during a three-day Management Boot Camp I facilitated for a mid-sized energy services company in central Vermont. From the start, he came across as focused and thoughtful—the kind of guy who takes pride in doing things right. He was sharp, contributed meaningfully in seminar sessions, and clearly cared about being a good leader.

After day one, Jake stayed behind, not with a specific question, but just to connect. There was something about his posture, like he was processing more than just the material. On day two, he lingered again. This time, he opened up.

"I don't know what it is," he said. "I've got this nagging feeling that something's off. I show up, I pull my weight, I think I'm doing the right things . . . but I'm just not breaking through with some of the team. It's like I'm missing something."

He wasn't looking for a shortcut. He was looking for clarity—why his effort with his team wasn't landing the way he hoped, and why certain moments with his crew felt just out of sync. There was a quiet tension beneath his confidence, the kind that shows up when you start questioning whether your perception of your leadership matches the experience others are having.

That conversation opened the door. The ABCD Model was a perfect fit for him. But when Jake couldn't answer questions about how his team experienced him as a leader and person, I knew he needed help self-assessing. So, I pointed him to the MADE Leadership Aptitude Assessment—not as a fix-all, but as a tool to help him explore what he might be missing. He took it that evening.

With eight critical leadership categories evaluated, Jake now had a clearer view of where he stood and what steps to take next.

Jake's MADE Leader Assessment Results at a Glance

Category	Score	Performance Level
Motivation	*4.8*	Exceptional Performance
Emotional Intelligence	*3.6*	Strong Capability
Self-Awareness	*3.0*	Shows Potential
Accountability	*4.1*	Strong Capability
Growth Mindset	*2.4*	Significant Growth Needed
Adaptability	*3.2*	Show Potential
Integrity	*4.5*	Exceptional Performance
Communication	*3.8*	Strong Capability

Total MADE Leader Score: 29.4 *(Developing Leader)*

Jake's Key Insights (Category Scores)

Exceptional Performance

- **Motivation (4.8)**
  Jake's *motivation* stood out as a leadership superpower. He was deeply driven by his passion for renewable energy and his desire to create a positive impact within his team. His natural enthusiasm inspired those around him.
  - *Insight*: Jake can leverage his high *motivation* to set ambitious goals and rally his team behind them. However, he must ensure this drive doesn't lead to

burnout by balancing it with practical planning.

- **Integrity (4.5)**
  Jake consistently aligned his actions with his values, earning the trust and respect of his team. His reliability set a standard for accountability and fairness.
  - *Insight*: Jake can use his strong sense of *integrity* to model ethical decision-making and foster a culture of trust within his organization.

Strong Capability

- **Emotional Intelligence (3.6)** and **Communication (3.8)**
  Jake demonstrated solid skills in understanding and managing emotions, both his own and others'. His communication was clear and effective in day-to-day operations.
  - *Insight*: By practicing active listening and seeking feedback more frequently, Jake can refine these areas into true standout strengths.
- **Accountability (4.1)**
  Jake reliably delivered on his commitments and expected the same from his team.
  - *Insight*: He could enhance team accountability by fostering an environment where others feel empowered to take ownership of their tasks.

Shows Potential

- **Self-Awareness (3.0)**
  Jake's score suggested room to deepen his understanding of how his actions and emotions affect others.
  - *Insight*: Journaling daily or seeking regular feedback from trusted colleagues could help Jake improve his *self-awareness*.
- **Adaptability (3.2)**
  Jake was somewhat flexible but struggled with navigating major changes, often defaulting to frustration or resistance.
  - *Insight*: Practicing mindfulness techniques and actively seeking challenges that require pivoting could help Jake embrace change more positively.

Significant Growth Needed

- **Growth Mindset (2.4)**
  Jake's score in this category indicated a tendency to view setbacks as failures rather than opportunities to learn.
  - *Insight*: Jake needs to reframe his mindset by focusing on progress over perfection. Regularly reminding himself and his team that mistakes are part of growth could transform his leadership approach.

Jake's Action Plan: Prioritizing Jake's Growth Areas

1. **Growth Mindset**
   As Carol Dweck explained in her book *Mindset*, a growth mindset is the belief that abilities can be developed through effort and learning—a principle Jake

embraced as he decided to focus here first, recognizing that shifting his perspective on challenges would create a ripple effect on his *adaptability* and *self-awareness.*

- *Action Step*: Jake committed to reflecting on a mistake each week, identifying one lesson he can carry forward.

2. **Adaptability**
   Jake set a goal to respond to unexpected changes with a solution-oriented attitude.
   - *Action Step*: During the next project shift, Jake will consciously practice seeing change as an opportunity and ask his team for input on adjustments.
3. **Self-Awareness**
   Jake planned to seek more regular feedback from his manager and peers.
   - *Action Step*: Jake scheduled monthly one-on-one check-ins with trusted colleagues to discuss how his leadership style was perceived.

A Word on Leveraging Strengths

Leveraging your strengths in the MADE Leader categories is essential for accelerating your growth. High-scoring areas aren't just evidence of what you do well—they're powerful tools to help you address areas where growth is needed. Your strengths provide a solid foundation of confidence and capability, giving you the momentum and mindset to tackle lower-scoring categories.

By building on what you already excel at, you create a strategic, strengths-based approach to balanced and effective leadership. Take Jake, for example:

Jake used his high *Motivation* to set a vision for the team's quarterly goals, framing them as a shared mission to drive company success.

With his strong *Integrity*, Jake led a cross-departmental project, reinforcing his reputation as a dependable and ethical leader.

Jake's Total MADE Leader Score of 29.4 placed him in the *Developing Leader* category, highlighting his solid capabilities while also pointing out his clear opportunities for growth. By focusing on improving his growth mindset and adaptability, Jake was well-positioned to advance into the *Strong Leader* range with dedicated time and effort.

No Excuses, No Limits: These Are Your Options

"I gotta make it or make it; these are the options."

I heard that lyric on the way to basketball practice while driving my son Jace and three of his Glenburn teammates. The song *(Options)* was by an artist I hadn't heard of—NF—and that line was the hook. The boys played the tune on repeat, drilling it into the belly of my mind. I was initially annoyed, but later, I was glad they did. It stuck with me. It pushed me.

That evening, I caught myself rapping it under my breath—at my desk, then again mid-rep while chest pressing at the gym. Music has a way of getting in your system. But that NF line wasn't just a vibe—it was a challenge. And challenge is fuel for growth.

For leaders, growth isn't optional. Neither is the work. The choice is simple: step up or stay stuck. If you choose to step up, the MADE system gives you the framework—and the fire—to do it. Both MADE options are built to help you claim your next level on your terms.

Now it's time for you to *make it or make it.*

The MADE assessment phase lays out two clear choices: Option 1 or Option 2. Below, we'll introduce these options and show how they work in real life through two examples of Jake's leadership journey.

Option 1: ***The Test-Retest Model*** lets you track your growth over time, putting your effort and progress under the spotlight. It's about proving to yourself—no fluff—that you're stronger today than you were yesterday.

Option 2: ***The Trusted Colleague-Partner Model*** brings an outside perspective into the mix, helping you uncover blind spots and challenge the way you see yourself. It's raw, it's real, and it's designed to make you better.

This is your roadmap to becoming the kind of leader others want to follow. There's no room for hesitation here—*just action, accountability,* and *results.* To illustrate how these options can drive real transformation, let's continue Jake's story and see how each one plays out in practice.

Fast Forward: Jake's Journey Paying Off – Option 1 and Option 2

Option 1 (The Test-Retest Model)

Jake took action!

After completing his initial MADE Leadership Assessment and reviewing his scores, Jake realized he needed to step up and make meaningful changes to become the leader his team needed. Armed with insights from the

MADE Leader Assessment results, his copy of *Win By 100*, and a commitment to his MADE Leader Action Plan, he spent the next three months focused on intentional growth. Jake followed a structured approach: he embraced weekly reflections to strengthen his *Growth Mindset*, used monthly one-on-one feedback sessions with his peers and manager to deepen his *Self-Awareness*, and actively reframed challenges as opportunities to improve his *Adaptability*. His goal wasn't perfection, but rather to achieve consistent progress in the areas the MADE assessment had highlighted for growth. After three months of focus on his leader development goals, Jake took the MADE assessment again. This time, the results told a compelling story of transformation. His Total MADE Leader Score rose from 29.4 to 32.7, elevating him from a "*Developing Leader*" to a "*Strong Leader.*" Below is a comparison of Jake's original scores and his retest scores:

MADE Category	**Jake's Original Score**	**Performance Level *(Original)***	**Jake's Reassessment Score**	**Performance Level *(Reassessment)***
Motivation	4.8	Exceptional Performance	4.8	Exceptional Performance
Emotional Intelligence	3.6	Strong Capability	3.8	Strong Capability
Self-Awareness	3.0	Shows Potential	4.0	Strong Capability
Accountability	4.1	Strong Capability	4.2	Strong Capability
Growth Mindset	2.4	Significant Growth Needed	3.4	Shows Potential
Adaptability	3.2	Shows Potential	4.0	Strong Capability
Integrity	4.5	Exceptional Performance	4.5	Exceptional Performance
Communication	3.8	Strong Capability	4.0	Strong Capability
Total MADE Leader Score	***29.4***	***Developing Leader***	***32.7***	***Strong Leader***

These scores reflected Jake's remarkable growth across critical leadership dimensions. His *Growth Mindset*, for example, rose a point from 2.4 to 3.4, showcasing how his commitment to viewing challenges as learning opportunities reshaped his perspective. His *Adaptability* jumped from 3.2 to 4.0 as he embraced change, involving his team more in problem-solving and turning uncertainty into innovation. Likewise, his *Self-Awareness* saw a dramatic full-point increase—from 3.0 to 4.0—fueled by consistent, honest feedback from peers and his manager, which gave him a clearer understanding of his leadership impact.

This *Test-Retest* model didn't just measure Jake's progress—it affirmed the resilience and determination he poured into becoming a more effective leader. By taking the MADE assessment twice, Jake could tangibly track his evolution and see how his efforts directly translated into stronger leadership performance. The transformation was about becoming a leader who inspires trust, fosters collaboration, and raises the bar for his entire team.

Jake's journey using the *Test-Retest* model proves that focused, intentional growth not only pays off but has the power to redefine leadership itself. The MADE assessment, combined with the practical Action Steps in the report, provided Jake with a clear roadmap for transformation. His dedication turned that roadmap into results, demonstrating that with the right tools, mindset, and perseverance, anyone can elevate their leadership to extraordinary levels.

Option 2: The Trusted Colleague-Partner Model

Let's say that instead of the *Test-Retest Model*, Jake decided to take the second approach to the MADE assessment by combining his self-assessment with feedback from someone he trusted.

After completing the assessment himself, Jake scored a Total MADE Leader Score of 29.4, placing him in the *Developing Leader* performance level. This gave him a clear view of his strengths, like *Motivation* (4.8) and *Integrity* (4.5), as well as growth areas, including *Growth Mindset* (2.4), *Adaptability* (3.2), and *Self-Awareness* (3.0).

However, Jake knew that self-awareness and leadership aren't just about how you see yourself. To gain an external perspective, Jake asked Maria, a trusted colleague who worked closely with him, to take the MADE assessment on his behalf and rate his leadership practices. He chose Maria because she had seen him in action during high-pressure situations and had consistently offered constructive feedback. He trusted she'd be truthful about how he came across as a leader.

When Jake compared his self-assessment with Maria's feedback, the differences were eye-opening and affirming.

MADE Category	Jake's Self-Assessment	Performance Level (Jake)	Maria's Assessment of Jake	Performance Level (Maria)
Motivation	4.8	Exceptional Performance	4.8	Exceptional Performance
Emotional Intelligence	3.6	Strong Capability	3.6	Strong Capability
Self-Awareness	3.0	Show Potential	3.0	Show Potential
Accountability	4.1	Strong Capability	4.2	Strong Capability
Growth Mindset	2.4	Significant Growth Needed	2.8	Show Potential
Adaptability	3.2	Show Potential	3.6	Strong Capability
Integrity	4.5	Exceptional Performance	4.5	Exceptional Performance
Communication	3.8	Strong Capability	4.0	Strong Capability
Total MADE Leader Score	**29.4**	***Developing Leader***	**30.5**	***Developing Leader***

Maria's Total MADE Leader Score for Jake came out slightly higher at 30.5, still within the *Developing Leader* range but providing a more balanced perspective of his leadership. By juxtaposing his own results with Maria's perception—both using the same lexicon and methodology—Jake uncovered invaluable insights into how others experienced his leadership versus how he saw himself. Additionally, the shared language of the MADE system gave Jake and Maria a mutual framework for future discussions about his growth and performance as a leader.

Guided by the MADE principles, Jake updated his development plan to target the areas Maria's feedback highlighted. He prioritized actions such as engaging his team in collaborative problem-solving, seeking consistent feedback from peers, and reframing challenges with a growth-oriented mindset. Over the next three months, Jake worked deliberately on these focus areas, regularly checking in with Maria and other colleagues to ensure his progress stayed on track.

By combining the MADE assessment with a trusted partner's perspective (Maria), Jake was able to uncover blind spots, validate his self-perception, and align his efforts with real feedback. This dual approach didn't just sharpen his self-awareness—it also strengthened the trust and collaboration within his team. The insights he gained from Option 2: The Trusted Colleague-Partner became the cornerstone of his leadership growth, helping him take targeted action to close the gap between how he saw himself and how others experienced his leadership.

Jake's Option 2 experience proves that effective leadership growth comes from looking inward while also being open to honest feedback from those you trust. By leveraging the Trusted Colleague-Partner option, he turned the MADE assessment into a transformative tool for understanding and improving his leadership impact.

Harnessing the Power of Self-Reflection and Trusted Feedback

Now we see all our earlier talk about feedback coming back around.

You're the director of this movie, and you've got two options of how you want to shoot this scene. Lucky for you, both paths of the MADE Leadership *assessment phase* are transformative approaches to understanding your leadership impact, so you can't choose wrongly. *But consider the following:*

Option 1: Test-Retest: Encourages honest, introspective self-reflection to identify your leadership strengths and areas for growth. You take the assessment twice—first as a baseline and later as a measure of progress after implementing the insights from the MADE principles.

Option 2: The Trusted Colleague-Partner: Combines your self-assessment with feedback from a trusted colleague, providing external perspectives that uncover blind spots and/or validate your self-perceptions.

Both options offer unique benefits for leadership growth, and you can choose the approach that best aligns with your goals.

Here's how to make the most of either path.

Step One: Start with Self-Assessment

Begin by taking the MADE self-assessment. This step establishes a baseline for your leadership capabilities through introspective reflection. Honest self-assessment is crucial for identifying where you stand and creating a focused plan for growth. Upon completion, you'll gain insights into your leadership that ignite a desire to improve and grow. You may even think of someone whose feedback could provide additional clarity and perspective. Most individuals who take the self-assessment find that choosing between Option 1 and Option 2 becomes clearer after first reflecting on their self-assessment results, making it easier to choose the path that aligns best with their leadership journey.

Step Two: Selecting Your Path

Option 1: Pure Test-Retest: After completing your initial self-assessment, dive into the Action Steps book and focus on areas for growth. Track your progress by taking the assessment again after implementing changes to your leadership approach. This retest provides tangible evidence of your development over time.

Option 2: The Trusted Colleague-Partner: After completing your self-assessment, invite a trusted colleague to take the MADE assessment on your behalf. Choose someone who interacts closely with you and can provide a balanced, honest perspective. This approach helps you identify blind spots and areas where your perception may differ from how others experience your leadership.

Step Three: Compare and Contrast

If you choose the **Trusted Colleague-Partner Option**, compare their assessment results with your own. Where do your self-perceptions align or differ from their observations? These comparisons reveal critical insights, validate strengths, and highlight key opportunities for growth.

Mark Twain gets credit for a lot of sharp one-liners he probably never said—and this is one of them: "It ain't what you don't know that gets you into trouble. It's what you know for sure that just ain't so." No verified source, but it doesn't matter. The message hits.

What we're convinced we've got handled is often what's hurting us most.

In leadership, that's your blind spot—the space between how you think you show up and how people actually experience you. And that gap can be where your biggest growth potential lives. The real danger isn't ignorance. It's certainty without clarity.

If you choose Option 1, finish the book and put your best foot forward with your MADE action plan. Once you feel like you have made considerable progress, retake the assessment to see how your results have changed. Compare and contrast the results from each assessment.

Both options in the MADE Leadership Aptitude Assessment empower you to turn insights into action. Whether tracking progress with **Option 1: The Pure Test-Retest** or gaining external perspectives with **Option 2: The Trusted Colleague-Partner**, the MADE system is your roadmap to measurable growth and transformation.

Choosing Your Approach: Comparing Option 1 and Option 2

Criteria	Option 1: Pure Test-Retest	Option 2: The Trusted Colleague-Partner
Source of Feedback	Solely your own perspective, reflecting your honest self-assessment.	Your self-assessment combined with feedback from a trusted colleague who knows you well.
Focus	Personal growth over time, measured by comparing your initial self-assessment to a follow-up after targeted efforts.	Understanding how your leadership is perceived externally versus your self-perception, highlighting blind spots and validating strengths.
Timeframe	A gap of three to six months between assessments to allow for measurable growth.	Conducted shortly after your initial self-assessment, focusing on alignment or misalignment between internal and external perceptions.
Insights Gained	Progress tracking: clear evidence of growth or stagnation based on changes in your scores.	A broader perspective: alignment, blind spots, and additional areas for development.
Self-Reflection Component	Requires you to evaluate your efforts and adjustments between assessments.	Encourages you to reflect on both your own scores and the trusted colleague's input for a richer understanding of your leadership.
Use Case	Ideal for leaders focused on introspection and tracking personal growth independently.	Perfect for leaders seeking external validation and diverse perspectives without relying on a full 360-degree feedback process.

Assessment Wrap – The MADE Learning Zone

Congratulations on Completing the Self-Assessment Phase! Every journey starts with a single step, and the first actionable step of the MADE leader journey is self-assessment. Whether you chose Option 1 (measuring your own progress over time) or Option 2 (juxtaposing your perception with a trusted colleague's feedback), you've gained unique insights into your strengths and areas for growth. This phase isn't just about knowing where you stand; it's about building the confidence to take meaningful action.

And let me tell you—taking that first step takes guts. It takes real courage to look in the mirror, seek feedback, and confront the truth about your own leadership. But you did it!

By completing the MADE Leadership Assessment, you've chosen self-awareness over *complacency* and *reflection* over *avoidance*. That's a bold move—and it sets you apart from the masses. Go ahead and beam a bit—most people avoid the mirror. You didn't.

But I've still got some tough news for you: The *real challenge* starts now. Now we are getting into the tough stuff. So, lace up your boots high and tight. We're wading into deep waters. Self-assessment is no small feat, but let's get real—what you've gained so far is just knowledge. But, frankly, knowledge—by itself—is *useless*.

I know, you've heard all the clichés: Knowledge is Power. Knowledge is Life. Knowledge is King. Guess what? It's all BS. Knowledge is none of those things. I've seen it play out too many times to count—people with high levels of knowledge still failing to deliver results. It's because knowledge doesn't change a thing.

ACTION does!

Not intentions.

Not talking about it.

Just action. Every time.

This is where MADE leadership separates the dreamers from the doers. It's not enough to *know* what to do—you've got to *apply* it. And MADE doesn't stop there. It demands something more: *you've got to call your shot.*

No lucky breaks. No accidental wins. (Like my wild bank shot at the pep rally.)

The best leaders don't just live in their heads. They live out front . . . out loud. But one of the hardest things you'll ever do is call your shot *before shooting it.*

To declare what you're going to do—aloud, on the record—means taking on the weight of accountability. That's terrifying for most people. But for real leaders, it's non-negotiable. Leadership is about earning trust, and trust is built through bold, decisive action.

You've uncovered challenges and strengths in the assessment process. The foundation is set.

Whether it's off the glass, nothing but net, or some wild trick shot . . . it's time to call your shot. Time to make your *Declaration* as a leader.

This isn't just bold—it's necessary.

And remember: If you're here, you're built for this.

7

Declaration – Power of Public Commitment

A leader's declaration is the moment the talk stops, and the work starts. It's the turning point where insight stops living in your head and starts shaping your behavior.

Declaration isn't about setting goals you hope to reach someday. It's about drawing a line in the sand. It's about saying out loud, "This is who I'm becoming—and I'm done pretending otherwise."

Whether you say it to your team, your mentor, your partner, or just your lonely self in the mirror, you're owning it. You're making it real.

Declaration is powerful when it's public. Leaders who make these declarations become role models. I've seen it time and again. They don't just talk about values—they embody them. A declaration turns a leader's goals into visible, shared commitments. You either *put up* or *shut up*.

So, think of your MADE Declaration as putting up a signpost for everyone to see. You're essentially saying, "This is the direction I'm headed, and I'm taking you with me." You become the example, the North Star that others look to for guidance.

It's a bold gesture that not only solidifies your commitment but also encourages others to hold you accountable for your actions (and your inaction).

Why Declare It?

In my mid-twenties, I found myself working as a tech at a drug and alcohol inpatient clinic in Bangor, Maine. It wasn't where I'd imagined my life going, but I was coming off a different occupational experience that was so emotionally draining that I didn't know if I'd ever fully recover.

Before the clinic, I'd been working in the Child Protective and Children's Services sectors of the Department of Health and Human Services for the State of Maine, covering cases in the Lewiston/Auburn area (one of the toughest areas in the state). It's a job that requires a kind of strength most people don't have. But I felt that I had it. Young and bold, I thought I was strong enough to withstand the repeated heartbreak that came with the role.

I was wrong.

There was this one case, one child. She wasn't supposed to matter more to me than the others, but she did. She was thirteen—too young to have lived through what she had, and too old to believe anyone could save her. Pain clung to her like a second skin. The system was a revolving door of rejection: no group home in Maine could take three siblings, and no foster family could handle them all together. For a year, I was state guardian for her and her two younger siblings, and I was her constant in a world that gave her nothing but chaos.

She broke through every wall I'd put up. I knew every detail of her story, and every scar that story had left on her.

When the day finally came for me to testify in court on her behalf, I didn't hold back. I was clear, firm, and professional: "This child and her siblings *cannot* go back with their father."

It wasn't just unsafe; it was *unimaginable*.

I knew the weight of my testimony would be enough. I believed in the power of the truth. And I trusted that my testimony would save her.

I was wrong.

The judge didn't see it my way. He ordered her to be returned to her father's care under the protection of a DHHS Safety Plan. I left that courtroom feeling helpless, but the worst was still to come.

Less than a month later, my phone rang. Some calls you brace for, even before they come. This was one of them. I already knew.

I had to go back to *that* house. Back to *her*. But this time, *it was different*. This time, it was worse. She hadn't just been neglected. She hadn't just been hurt. She had been *broken* in the ugliest, most unthinkable way.

By the time I pulled up, two sheriffs were already there, their faces carved from stone, the kind of men who had seen too much, who had been here before. This wasn't their first visit to this house. Probably wouldn't be their last.

And then I saw her.

She was standing outside, just past the crumbling porch, beneath the flickering glow of a half-dead floodlight. She was shaking. Her arms locked around her own body, like she was trying to hold herself together. Her face was streaked with dirt, cheap makeup, and tears, but her eyes—my God, her eyes. They weren't just sad. They were *empty*.

I ran to her, my heart in a heap.

This time she didn't reach for me. She didn't flinch. She didn't even blink.

She just looked at me, like someone who had run out of ways to fight, or reasons to care. And then, with a voice so filled with pain that it barely belonged to her anymore, she said something I'll never forget—something that still crawls into my mind some nights.

"The only reason I haven't killed myself is because of them. My little sisters. They're all I have. You promised me you'd help them, and you didn't. You promised!"

She cried harder then. And I swear I felt the ground shift beneath me. Because right then, I knew. This wasn't just *a moment.* It wasn't just *another* case, *another* terrible story, *another* kid I had to pull from a hell they never deserved. This was the edge of her cliff. And if I didn't do something—if I didn't *hold on to her*—she was going over.

I swallowed the lump in my throat. Took a breath that felt like swallowing glass. This was her line. And I had made a declaration to protect her that I hadn't delivered on.

Two days later, back at court, the same judge who had sent her back to her father was now shattering what little lifeline she had left.

Deemed "a danger to herself" and with no available beds to support suicidal teens in Maine, the judge ordered her to a mental health institution three hundred miles away in Vermont—ripping her from the only family she had left. Her little sisters were placed in foster homes back in central Maine, not just separated from *her*, but from *each other.*

My heart broke for them. My heart broke for her.

She was barely thirteen, and already, the world had taken *everything.*

As her caseworker and state guardian, it was my job to take her three hundred miles out-of-state to a mental health facility in the mountains of Vermont. More than half of the drive was filled with her sobs and moans, broken pleas to stay with her sisters, and a heartbreak so loud it drowned out the sound of the road.

I tried to stay composed, but inside, I was unraveling. Every mile felt heavier—like the car was dragging the weight of everything she'd been through.

When I finally left her at the facility, she clung to my arm, pulled so hard she ripped my shirt. (*I still have it.*) She was begging me not to go. Her tears soaked through my sleeve. And then I had to just . . . leave her there.

Alone.

I'm typing through tears right now. To this day, I can't even think about that moment without crying. It still makes me burn with an anger I don't know where to put.

The drive back to Maine was silent—except for my own sobs. I pleaded with God the whole way, shouting through the empty car, begging Him to protect her.

"She's just a baby," I kept saying. "How is this her life? How is this anyone's life?"

I knew then that I couldn't do it anymore. The job was killing me. But leaving wasn't as simple as walking away. The guilt followed me like a shadow. I couldn't shake the feeling that I had abandoned her, that she was my responsibility, and I had let her down. It sank me into my own depression.

Ironically, that weekend, my college friend and mentor, Donald Crump—*DC* to me—showed up from North Carolina for a visit. The moment he saw me, he just stood there, arms crossed, studying me like a man taking inventory of something broken. Finally, he shook his head.

"What happened to you?"

At first, I brushed it off. But he wasn't talking about my job, my stress, or my exhaustion—he meant *me*. Said my spirit, the fire, the man I used to be, was just *gone*.

"You're not the same, TJ. Not even close. Your face looks kinda the same, but I barely recognize you."

DC had known me since undergrad, at Pfeiffer University. Back when I still had light in my eyes, when I could shake off the hard days instead of letting them sink into my bones. But now he could see what I refused to admit to myself—this work was pulling me under.

He told me the truth and didn't sugarcoat it: "You can't help anyone if you're falling apart, TJ. And you're falling apart. You have to take care of yourself, too, man."

I didn't want to hear it. But deep down, I knew DC was right.

Monday morning. 8:00 AM.

I didn't resign—I quit.

Not the polished kind. Not the "thank you for the opportunity" kind. I quit because I couldn't breathe in that place one more day.

Resigning is what you do when you're calm, collected, and ready to move on. Quitting is what you do when staying feels like self-betrayal.

Resigning is letting go.

Quitting is about survival.

If you've ever had to quit something that was killing your spirit, you already know.

Quitting isn't weakness.

It's finally *choosing you.*

It was time to reclaim that person that DC told me I still had in me somewhere—the one I had to refuse to leave behind.

I packed up my apartment in Auburn, stuffing pieces of my life into half-crushed Chiquita banana boxes like they didn't matter. But they did. Every scrap, every object carried a memory—a reminder of what I saw, what I held, what I tried to fix and couldn't. I left it all behind. But the weight of it all? That came with me.

I drove nearly two hours north to Bangor, no job, no plan, just a trunk full of whatever fit, and a head full of noise. What *now*? What *next*? I had no answers.

Rodney and Tess, my only married and somewhat-settled friends, let me crash in their basement. I told them (and myself) it was "extremely temporary," but deep down, I didn't know if that was true. That first night, I lay on their pull-out couch, staring at the low basement ceiling, listening to the deep hum of the furnace and the click of it kicking on, kicking off. The air was stiff, the kind that settles deep into the space and walls of unfinished basements—damp, stale, unmoving.

I was a grown man, sleeping in a friend's basement. No job. No direction. No fire left. I wasn't just broke. *I was broken.*

Desperation drove me to send out résumés to *anyone* who would take a look at me. I wasn't picky. I wasn't proud. I just needed something—*anything*—to climb out of the hole I was in. That's when Bill Rae called me back after seeing my résumé. He ran Manna Inc., a local drug and alcohol clinic, and got straight to the point:

"Are you serious about *helping people*?"

"*Helping people?*" The way he phrased it stopped me cold. I didn't know how to answer that. It felt like a loaded question. Could I even claim to be serious about *helping people* after the way my last helping role had ended? After the way I felt like I had failed to help a vulnerable little girl?

But I swallowed my doubt, shoved my guilt aside, and told him, "Yes . . . yes, sir."

I was broke as a joke—hot dogs and ramen on repeat, already crashing in Rod and Tess's basement. So, with my pride, my purpose, and my back against the wall, I headed to meet Mr. Rae for my official interview. He extended his hand and introduced himself. “I’m Pastor Rae.”

I hadn’t expected that. But my dad was a pastor, too, and maybe that familiarity cracked something open in me, made me let my guard down just enough to tell him the truth—*all* of it.

He didn’t flinch. Instead, he leaned in, met my eyes, and asked a question that caught me completely off guard.

“Can I pray for you?”

For a second, I just sat there, stunned. I wasn’t sure what prayer could do for me at that point, wasn’t convinced it would change *anything*. But in that moment? I was willing to try it. I just wanted my life to get better and to mean something. So I nodded.

He prayed. I wept.

I started on Monday.

The Power of Showing Up

I didn’t know anything about addiction recovery, so my role was basic: intake forms, making small talk, “helping people,” and getting them to settle in. I was learning that sometimes, it’s the smallest gestures that make the biggest difference for people. I started to like the job, and my responsibilities grew with my knowledge as the weeks went by. Eventually, I gained Pastor Rae’s trust, along with a new mid-week responsibility that would completely change the way I look at life.

Every Wednesday, my job changed. Pastor Rae handed me the keys to the Manna van, trusting me to load it up with our patients, and drive them to Bangor Baptist Church for an Alcoholics Anonymous (AA) meeting. I had no idea what to expect that first time. Just a church basement, a circle of strangers, and stories I wasn't sure I was meant to hear. But I quickly realized something: those meetings weren't just gatherings. They were sacred.

My role was simple—fill cups with lemonade, pass around cookies, sit in the back, and stay quiet. No fixing. No judging. Just *be there.*

And as I sat there with them, week after week, something inside me started shifting, too. I watched real people stripped down to their rawest selves stand up and own their stories. No filters. No rehearsed speeches. Just brutal, unvarnished truth.

"This is who I am . . .

this is what I've done . . .

and this is what I'm fighting."

Some spoke with voices steady as stone. Others cracked wide open, words shaking, hands trembling. But no matter how they said it, they said it. And there was power in that. Power in *admitting.* Power in *acknowledging.*

At the time, I didn't see it yet, but those meetings weren't just about addiction. They were about *leadership***.** Because leadership isn't about having all the answers. It's not about perfection or control. It's about stepping up—flawed, vulnerable, and honest—and saying, "This is where I am. And I'm willing to do the work to make things better."

The Moment of Declaration

The first thing I noticed was the weight many people carried when they walked in the door. You could tell when it was someone's first meeting. They sat with their arms crossed, or looking down, anything to make themselves small. There was fear in their eyes—and desperation too. These were people who had hit what many call "rock bottom." Their consequences had piled up so high they couldn't see a way out.

At first, most barely spoke. Some stayed completely silent, eyes down, shoulders slumped, lost somewhere deep inside themselves. But week after week, I watched. And if you paid close enough attention, you could see it—*the shift*.

Maybe it was subtle. A slight change in posture. Someone sitting up a little straighter. A knee bouncing with a new nervous energy. Their eyes darting around the room, finally *seeing* the people around them instead of just staring at the floor.

After a few weeks of witnessing, I always knew when it was coming. It was in the way they inhaled a little too deeply, exhaled a little too slowly. The way their hands clenched, then released. The way their mouths paused, then parted—like the words were right there, stuck just behind their lips, waiting for permission.

But then, finally—it would just happen.

A voice, shaky but determined, breaking through the silence.

The first step. The moment they stopped holding it in and started letting it go.

They'd stand up. Hands trembling. Shoulders curled in like they wanted to disappear. Eyes darting, searching for an escape that couldn't exist.

And then the words would come.

"Hi, my name is ______, and I'm an alcoholic."

Just like that, the entire room would move.

It was no longer just *their* burden. No longer a secret choking the life out of them. They weren't running from it anymore. They'd *owned it*. And you could see it—the relief and the terror, colliding on their faces like two storms meeting in the middle.

And then came the flood.

The shaky voice trying to hold steady.
The breath—hitching, catching, breaking.
Then, the tears.

Spilling out, mixing with the kind of raw, running snot that only shows up when the heart cracks in two. The trembling hands, gripping the edge of a folding chair like it was the only thing holding them to earth.

It was raw. It was messy.

And it was absolutely beautiful.

But here's what really got me. As soon as those words left their mouth, the room came alive. Chairs scraped against the scratched-up floor tiles as people stood quickly to clap and praise them. Onlookers ran to them, pulling them into tight, all-too-knowing embraces. Voices, steady and certain, spoke up:

"You're doing it."

"You're not alone."

"You've got this, sweetie. It's okay! We've got you."

I bet for a lot of them, it was the first time in a long time they'd heard words like that. The first time they'd felt seen. Felt love. Felt support that didn't come with strings or shame.

Most had burned their families out years ago—casualties of the slow crash toward rock bottom. They were used to being looked past, not looked in the eye. But here, at their declaration, people finally said to them, "You're worth fighting for."

Watching that happen week after week taught me something profound about people. That act of standing up and declaring their truth wasn't just a ritual—it was a *threshold.* It was the moment where fear turned into courage and shame turned into possibility.

At the time, I was just a kid myself—twenty-five, maybe twenty-six years old. I thought I had a pretty good sense of the world, but turns out, I didn't know squat. Sitting in that room, watching people unravel their pain in front of strangers, I realized just how much courage it takes to face yourself.

Each declaration was a key that unlocked doors people thought were sealed shut forever. I watched it happen over and over, as men and women who had spent years running finally stood still and spoke their truth. And in doing so, they stepped into something they never thought they deserved: freedom.

The Challenge for You

The Declaration in MADE is about more than just the words. It's about stepping into accountability, vulnerability, and transformation. Those people in the AA meetings didn't just admit their struggles—they owned them, out loud, in front of others. And that real ownership? That's the first meaningful step toward change.

Declaration isn't just for people in recovery. It's for anyone ready to stop hiding, stop minimizing, and start owning the work ahead. Your declaration might look different, but the principle is the same. It's the moment you stop wishing and start committing.

Life doesn't get real until you get real. Those people I saw in AA gatherings weren't magically fixed after standing up and saying a few brave words. They had a long, arduous road of recovery ahead of them—but they took the one step that actually matters.

The first one.

They stood up.

They owned their crap. (And truthfully, that's always respectable.)

So, what are you hiding from? What do you need to say out loud, to yourself, your spouse, your team, your mama, your boss, or anyone else?

Don't give me the "I'm not ready" excuse. Because you'll never *feel* ready. That's not how any of this works.

Just stand up.

Say it.

And let the work begin.

8

Declaration – Anchored In Psychology

Leadership isn't only about results—it's about the promises you make to get there. And let's be clear: your words as a leader carry weight. When you make a declaration, you're not just throwing out some vague intention like "I'll try to be better" or "We'll work on that." You're planting a flag. You're saying, "This is what I'm going to do, and you can hold me to it." That kind of boldness gets attention, and it builds trust.

But declaration is more than just protecting your reputation. It's about focus. That's where *cognitive anchoring* comes in. When you state your goal clearly and commit to it, you're not just sending a message to your team—you're sending one to your own brain. Your mind starts working differently. Instead of wasting energy on distractions, it zeros in on what matters most. In the workplace, that kind of clarity is priceless. "We'll improve team communication" isn't a declaration. It's fluff. "We'll implement weekly one-on-ones by next quarter to make sure every team member is aligned and supported"—that's a declaration. It demands action.

And let's not ignore the power of *social contracts.* When you make a bold statement in front of your team—whether it's in a meeting, an email, or a company-wide presentation—you're not just accountable to yourself anymore. You're accountable to them. That's leadership in its rawest form. You're showing your people that you don't just talk—you act. And when your team sees you step up, they're more likely to do the same. It creates a ripple effect. It changes the culture.

So, let's stop pretending that quiet goals and private intentions are enough. If you're serious about leading, you need to declare it. *Out loud.* To your team. To your peers. To your family. To whoever needs to be listening. Because leadership without accountability isn't leadership—it's a waste of everyone's time. A true declaration isn't just a statement; it's a promise backed by action. And if you're not ready to back it up, don't bother making it.

Declaration Versus Goal Setting

A declaration isn't the same as setting a goal. Goals are great—they give you direction. But how many goals have you set that you never hit? It's not because you didn't want them badly enough. It's because goals, on their own, are weak. They sit there on paper, looking nice and tidy, while life happens around them.

A declaration is a completely different beast. Goals are private. They live in notebooks, vision boards, or quiet convos with your boss. Declarations are public. They're loud. They're risky. They're specific. Once you say it out loud, it's not just about you anymore—it becomes a commitment.

Declarations also raise the stakes in leadership in ways goals don't. Your team isn't inspired by a half-hearted goal buried in your notebook.

Goals might get you *thinking*, but declarations get you *moving.* And the more you move, the more momentum you build—for yourself and everyone watching.

But there is a catch . . . a declaration is only as strong as *the process* behind it. If it's vague, rushed, or poorly thought out, it'll crumble under the weight of reality. To make a declaration that sticks, you need to build it the right way. Let's break it down step by step.

The Mechanics of a Powerful Declaration

A great declaration doesn't happen by accident. It's crafted with *intention* and backed by a *clear process*. Think of it like building a house: if the foundation isn't solid, the whole thing collapses. Here's how to lay that foundation with the staying power that you and your followers deserve.

Step 1. Start with Clarity

Vagueness kills momentum. If your declaration isn't specific, it's easy to wiggle out of when things get tough. Instead, get crystal *clear* about what you're committing to.

To help, I developed the C.L.E.A.R. framework *(Concrete, Linked, Executable, Accountable, Recordable)* for MADE system users to ensure that our declarations are always actionable, impactful, and time-bound. Declarations must not be vague wishes—they must be clear commitments that drive results.

Poor Declaration: *"I will improve team communication."* This is *not* a declaration—it's wishful thinking. There's no clear action, no accountability, and no timeline. It lacks most of the elements of the C.L.E.A.R. framework.

Solid Declaration: *"I will hold a fifteen-minute team huddle every Monday at 9 a.m. for the next three months, where each team member will provide a quick update on their priorities and challenges. Meeting notes will be documented to track progress, ensuring alignment and collaboration among all members of the team."*

This second example is a C.L.E.A.R. declaration because it's precise, time-bound, and leaves no room for ambiguity. It moves from an idea to an action that can be executed and measured. If a declaration isn't specific enough to act on *immediately,* it's not a declaration—it's just a thought. Seek to be *CLEAR*.

Letter	Meaning	Description
C	**Concrete**	The declaration is *specific* and leaves no room for ambiguity or interpretation.
L	**Linked**	It's *connected* to a meaningful goal or purpose, keeping it relevant and motivating.
E	**Executable**	Action steps are clear and *achievable*, defining exactly what needs to be done.
A	**Accountable**	A *system for follow-through* ensures progress, like sharing it or setting regular progress reviews.
R	**Recordable**	It's *documented*—written down or saved—*with metrics and a timeline* to make it visible and trackable.

Let's break down how the Solid Declaration example from above follows the CLEAR framework.

"I will hold a fifteen-minute team huddle every Monday at 9 a.m. for the next three months, where each team member will provide a quick update on their priorities and challenges. Meeting notes will be documented to track progress, ensuring alignment and collaboration among all members of the team."

Concrete – The declaration is specific and leaves no room for ambiguity.

- It explicitly states what will happen (a structured, fifteen-minute weekly team huddle).
- When: Every Monday at 9 a.m.
- For how long: The next three months.
- Why: To ensure alignment and collaboration among all team members.
- What will be covered: Each team member will share a quick update on their priorities and challenges.
- How it will be documented: Meeting notes will be taken for tracking progress.
- There's no vagueness—anyone reading this knows exactly what's being committed to and what to expect.

Linked – It's connected to a meaningful goal or purpose.

- The declaration isn't just about meetings—it explicitly states that the huddles will serve a purpose: keeping team members aligned and fostering collaboration.
- The focus on team priorities and challenges ensures that discussions stay relevant to the team's productivity and shared objectives.

- This strengthens the connection to broader business goals like *efficiency, communication, and team cohesion.*

Executable – Action steps are clear and achievable.

- Holding a fifteen-minute meeting at a consistent time every week is realistic and can be easily incorporated into the team's workflow.
- The structure—each person providing a quick update on priorities and challenges—ensures that the meeting stays focused and actionable.
- The three-month commitment makes it manageable and prevents it from feeling like an overwhelming or open-ended obligation.

Accountable – A system for follow-through is built in.

- The weekly repetition creates an automatic accountability system, so team members know how to prepare for and participate in the huddle.
- Since everyone is expected to provide updates, participation is reinforced as a team norm.
- The leader can track participation, engagement, and effectiveness over time, ensuring the commitment remains active.

Recordable – It's documented and trackable.

- The declaration is written down, making it a clear commitment.
- Trackable elements include:
    - Weekly frequency (every Monday).
    - Specific duration (fifteen minutes).
    - Defined timeframe (three months).

- Meeting notes ensure that discussions, challenges, and priorities are documented, making progress measurable.
- At the end of three months, the team can review the notes to evaluate whether the huddles improved alignment and collaboration, creating a natural reflection and improvement cycle.

Step 2. Write It Down (Record It)

This is somewhat built-in to the R (Recordable) in CLEAR, but it is important enough to be mentioned in isolation. Some declarations are deeply personal—you might not be ready or willing to share them with others yet, not even your spouse or your most trusted colleague. But to meet the standard of a MADE-style declaration, you need to take it out of your head and bring it into the real world. So, write it down—on paper, record it in a note on your phone, or in a document on your computer.

There's power in writing. It turns a fleeting thought into something tangible—a commitment you can see and feel. Once it's written, keep it visible: post it on your desk, save it as your phone's lock screen, or share it in a workspace where your team can see it. Visibility breathes life into your commitment and keeps it top of mind.

Writing can also help refine your message. It gives you the space to get the *wording just right* before you share it with your spouse, your team, or others. The right diction matters—clarity and precision take time, but they're worth it. A well-crafted declaration carries weight and leaves no doubt about what you stand for.

Finally, include clear metrics with a due date or expiration date. Specify exactly what you plan to do and when, and provide details like frequency, intensity, or duration. Metrics ensure your intentions are concrete, leaving no room for ambiguity about what others can expect from you moving forward.

Step 3. Choose Your Audience Wisely

If your declaration is shareable, *choose wisely who you share it with.* A declaration gains strength when shared with the *right people*—those who truly matter. Select individuals who will hold you accountable, support you, and challenge you to stay on track. These aren't the ones who'll let you off the hook with a pat on the back; they're the ones who'll ask, "How's that declaration coming along?"

Brené Brown's concept of the "Square Squad" comes to mind here. In her #1 *New York Times* bestseller *Dare to Lead*, Brown doesn't sugarcoat it. She drops an atomic truth bomb that too many people ignore: "Not everyone deserves a front-row seat to your journey."

She challenges us to stop giving airtime to the wrong voices and focus on the select few—"those who have earned the right to hear our story."

And she doesn't hold back: "If you're not in the arena also getting your a** kicked, I'm not interested in your feedback."

When I read that, my heart skipped a beat. I felt that. *Hard.*

I'd spent way too much time letting people chirp from the sidelines in my own game of life—feeling like I owed them my attention, my energy. I thought I was being arrogant if I didn't at least listen to every person who felt inclined to offer advice or weigh in on my path. Some wore nice suits. Some had titles. Some stood in front of classrooms. Some had a full head of gray hair. But when I started thinking about it the way Brown put it—how many of those people had *actually* been in the fight? How many had put themselves on the line, taken real risks, built something from nothing? Just because someone talks like an expert doesn't mean they've lived what you're living. And if they haven't been in it—*really in it*—then maybe they don't know what's best for you after all. Besides, who said gray hairs always equal wisdom?

The reason her message hit me so hard wasn't just because it was true—it was because *I* saw *myself* in it. Because early in my teaching career, I was one of those people.

I remember standing in front of undergraduate students, teaching business classes at a community college, telling them how to navigate corporate environments—despite the fact that I had *never* worked in that environment myself; I'd *never* held a corporate leadership role. At that point, the closest I had gotten to corporate was scanning canned goods at a large retailer. And yet, there I was, *acting* like I had the blueprint.

And the worst part? The longer you pretend, the more you believe your own lie.

It's not only experience that changes you. It's repetition, too. Say something enough times, and it starts to feel like the truth—*even when it isn't*. You stop questioning yourself. You stop checking your own qualifications. Stop grading your own paper. You get comfortable in the false confidence of knowing the words—without ever knowing the weight of the work.

That's the danger.

There's a difference between *knowing the script* and *knowing the struggle.* A difference between talking about the climb and actually making it to the top. And when it comes to advice—especially the kind that shapes your career, your relationships, your future—you better make sure the person in your ear has actually been where you're trying to go. Not where *they* went back in the '80s. Not what worked *back then.* Because let's be honest—what looked like courage in the '80s might get you canceled, crushed, or fired in 2026.

Not every voice deserves your attention. In all honesty, there are some educated dummies out here—clueless PhDs, cloudy CEOs, even a few politicking preachers running game in the name of God. Just because someone talks slick, dresses nice, or stands on a stage doesn't mean they've earned the right to speak into your life.

Be careful who you let influence you. Titles don't mean truth. Suits don't mean substance. And a mic doesn't make someone a mentor. Because when the storm hits and your back's against the wall—some of these folks will be missing . . . others will be just as lost, just as unsure, and just as in the dark as you are—but skilled at acting like they know best.

It's not enough to just be in the *area.* You need to know if they've been in the *arena.*

Area to Arena? That "n" makes a big difference.

In research, *n* stands for population size.

But in this case? That n equals credibility.

And even that's not good enough sometimes. Because being in the *arena* is one thing—but did they take the hits? Did they stay when it got bloody? Did they get back up after getting knocked down?

If they haven't sacrificed for it, struggled through it, or come out the other side with some scars—then what they're saying isn't guidance. It's just noise.

That's where your Square Squad comes in. These are the people who have earned their voice in your life. The ones who have been in the trenches *with you, for you, alongside you*. The ones who don't back down when things get hard. The ones who *call you out* when you're slacking and *push you harder* when you're winning.

They don't just talk. They show up. They fight. And if they haven't been in the fight or stood in your corner without question, their opinion doesn't count. *Period.*

So, don't reduce your declaration to a social media post, and be sure it isn't up for debate. Sharing it with the *wrong* people—those who don't understand your vision, don't respect your grind, and wouldn't put in the work themselves—*only waters down your commitment.* It invites doubt, distraction, and opinions that don't matter.

Instead, share it with the few who will hold you to it. The ones who demand the best from you, who won't let you off the hook, and who will call you out if you start playing small. Because declarations aren't for applause. They're for *executing.*

Step 4. Pair It with Visualization

Visualization primes your brain for action. That isn't fluff—it's neuroscience.

Spend a few minutes picturing what success looks like. Imagine the meeting where you deliver on your promise. See the look on your team's faces when they know you've followed through. Feel the satisfaction of crossing that finish line.

As author and speaker Dr. Denis Waitley is often quoted as saying, "When you visualize, then you materialize. If you've been there in the mind, you'll go there in the body." This idea aligns with a powerful truth: visualization creates a conflict in your brain between what is and what could be. Your mind works to resolve that conflict by taking action toward the vision.

By visualizing success, you're essentially rehearsing for it. You're training your mind to believe in the outcome—and belief is what fuels the behavior to make it happen.

Step 5. Set Checkpoints for Accountability

Big commitments can be overwhelming. It's easy to declare something bold and then feel paralyzed by the sheer size of the task. That's why checkpoints are your secret weapon. They break your declaration into manageable chunks and help you stay on course. Without them, you're flying blind.

Think of checkpoints like mile markers in a marathon or waypoints on a mountain hike—they help you track progress and stay motivated. I experienced this firsthand during a memorable trip to Katahdin (the highest peak in Maine, and the northernmost terminus of the Appalachian Trail) while working as a resident director at Husson University in Bangor, Maine.

At the time, I had taken the job to maintain employee status, which allowed me to take free classes and afford a master's degree without piling up student loans. The hike was one of the perks of the role, and I joined a group of resident assistants, including a few football players, on the climb. Most of them were considerably younger than me, and while the football players seemed to sprint effortlessly up the trail, I found myself huffing and puffing, struggling to keep pace.

Panting like a thirsty dog, bent forward with my hands on my knees, I'd look north toward the peak. It seemed like north just kept getting norther. The peak looked impossibly far every time I glanced up, and it felt like I'd never make it. That's when I noticed the checkpoints along the trail. From that point, I stopped fixating on the summit and focused instead on just getting to *the next checkpoint*. Each one gave me something manageable to aim for and, when I reached one, a moment to micro-celebrate—a quick pause to catch my breath and acknowledge the progress I'd made. The checkpoints were indicators, evidence that I was progressing despite how I felt. Those mini celebrations gave me the motivation I needed to tackle the next stretch.

In leadership, checkpoints are like those progress markers; they're not optional; they're essential for keeping everyone aligned and on track. When you skip checkpoints, you risk wandering off course without even realizing it. And you risk demotivating your team.

Let's say your declaration is: *"By [specific date six months from now], our team will improve collaboration by fully implementing a project management system that streamlines communication, enhances task tracking, and increases overall efficiency."*

That's a big task—so break it down into clear checkpoints:

- One-Month Mark: Finalize the system selection *(research, compare, and choose the best fit).*
- Three-Month Mark: Ensure the team is fully trained and onboarded onto the system.

- Five-Month Mark: Review team performance metrics to see if collaboration is improving.
- Six-Month Mark: Evaluate success: Test it. Has collaboration improved? If not, what needs adjusting *(while there is still time)*?

This works because it keeps you focused and accountable with clear milestones. It prevents your objective from becoming another forgotten aspiration. It turns vision into action—one step at a time.

And don't underestimate the emotional power of checkpoints, too. Every time you hit one, it's an opportunity to celebrate progress—not just for you, but for your team. Small wins build momentum and remind everyone why the work matters. Peter Drucker famously said, "What gets measured gets managed . . . " By setting clear checkpoints and measuring your progress, you're not just managing the task—you're managing trust, engagement, and morale.

Transparency is key here. When you hit a personal checkpoint, share your progress with a trusted colleague or partner—someone who genuinely supports your growth and will challenge you when needed. Let them see that you're not just talking about leadership—*you're living it.* Their feedback can also give you insights you might have missed and keep you grounded in the bigger picture.

The key is to make your checkpoints specific and tied to tangible outcomes. Checkpoints keep you on track but missing one doesn't mean failure—it just means you need to adjust. When I missed a checkpoint on Katahdin, the summit didn't move. The peak wasn't any higher or lower just because I missed a signpost.

The same is true for leadership. Checkpoints are guides, not ultimatums. If you miss one, don't panic—simply recalculate, refocus, and keep climbing. Success isn't about hitting every checkpoint perfectly—it's about making sure you still reach the peak.

Case Studies: Real-Life Declarations (Work and Personal)

Declarations become real only when we see them in action. It's one thing to talk about bold commitments—it's another to watch them play out in the real world. Let me give you two examples, one from the trenches of leadership and one that's more personal, to show how declarations can drive transformation in either world.

The Casino GM Who Turned the Tables

I met Austin Muchemore at Hollywood Casino in Bangor, Maine, in 2022. From the moment I walked into his office, I could tell—*this GM cared.*

It wasn't just about running a casino. He was all about his people. The way he spoke about his team made one thing clear: he wasn't just managing a business—*he was building something bigger.* He wanted his people to grow, to succeed, and to take pride in their work.

Austin put it plainly—he wasn't there just to oversee operations. He was there to create something lasting. And he wasn't interested in winning alone—he wanted his *entire team to win* with him. Hollywood Casino was already a good place to work, but this GM saw something more—an opportunity to make it even better. He wasn't interested in maintaining the status quo. He wanted to build a workplace people were genuinely *proud to be part of.*

One day, during one of our 1:1 sessions, Austin made a declaration. He was resolute and determined in his tone and diction, so I recorded what he said in my notes. His declarative statement was neither vague nor overly aspirational, but still we talked about it and refined it until it was clear. By the end, this was it:

"In one year, Hollywood Casino will be a place where employees feel valued, engaged, and proud to work. We will achieve this by strengthening leadership connections, enhancing training, and improving communication, ensuring that our team's success drives an exceptional guest experience."

And he didn't stop there. He kept talking, conceptually building a roadmap. As he did, I could see the fire in his eyes—this wasn't just some dream to him . . . Austin had a *plan*. And every ounce of the man that is Austin Muchemore planned to make his ideas come to fruition.

After crafting his declaration, the first thing Austin did was meet with his leadership team. I facilitated the first of those meetings, and let me tell you, it was powerful. They all dug deep—not just into what could be improved, but into what was already working and how to make it even stronger. They asked big questions:

- How do we grow genuine trust among our team?
- How do we make sure our best people stay and thrive?
- How do we create an environment where employees feel valued and engaged?
- How do we take the guest experience to the next level?

Austin set a two-month checkpoint to roll out an anonymous employee feedback system. "If my people don't feel safe telling the truth," he told me, "I'll never get to the root of what we need to do next."

By month three, Austin was working closely with his HR Director, Kim Jenkins, to launch a new training program that was miles ahead of anything they'd done before. He asked me to consult with Kim and help her, and I was happy to do so.

From the start, it was clear that Kim was a rare kind of HR leader—the kind who didn't see professional development as a box to check but as the foundation of a thriving workplace. She understood that real growth happens beyond technical skills—it happens in *leadership*, in *trust*, and in the way *teams come together* to create unforgettable guest experiences. I grew a tremendous respect for Kim working with her and her team. She is a *glue-like* leader at the casino, the one who holds it all together.

But what stood out even more was that she wasn't pushing for change alone. Too often, HR leaders are tasked with driving culture, engagement, and training initiatives without real buy-in from executive or senior leadership peers (even the GM or CEO). They advocate for their people, but without strong executive support, their impact is limited. That wasn't the case here. Austin wasn't just approving the initiative—he was actively invested in it. He and Kim weren't working in silos; they were moving in sync, committed to building something stronger together.

As we built the training and development program, I saw the power of that alignment. Kim had the expertise, and Austin had the authority to make things happen. He didn't treat this as an *HR initiative*—he saw it as a *business priority.*

I know because I remember him telling me, "This isn't just training. It's a reset. We're giving our people the tools to be even better at what they already do well." That mindset made all the difference.

But the part that hit me hardest was how personal he made it. Austin declared that he would meet with every department lead biweekly, no exceptions. He didn't delegate it—he owned it himself. I asked him how he had time for it all, and he just laughed. "TJ, if I can't show up for them, how can I expect them to show up for me?"

And man, did they show up.

One year later, I walked back into the Hollywood Casino in Bangor, and the difference was undeniable. After months of intentional focus on leadership, team development, and guest experience, employee satisfaction scores had jumped by more than 20 percent—a new all-time high. Guest experience ratings had also hit their highest levels in years. But more than the numbers, you could feel the shift in the energy of the place. Employees weren't just doing their jobs—they were engaged, invested, and proud to be part of something bigger. But here's what stuck with me. It wasn't just the numbers that changed—it was the people.

One team member, Melissa McRae *(*the casino's Compliance Manager*)* pulled me aside while I was packing up my computer after a Leadership Journey session I'd facilitated for a group of emerging leaders. She said something that summed it all up: "This isn't just a job anymore. I'm proud to be here. I feel like I'm part of something here."

The moment she said it, I felt it hit me. Her words weren't just a passing comment. They were almost *word for word* what Austin had *declared* nearly a year earlier—his vision for what Hollywood Casino in Bangor would become.

"In one year, Hollywood Casino will be a place where employees feel valued, engaged, and proud to work."

And now? It wasn't just a vision—*it was real.*

That's the difference a great leader makes. When someone like Austin doesn't just talk about change—but lives it and invests in it, every single day—people don't just work harder. They believe deeper. They *buy in.* And when people believe in something bigger than a paycheck, when they feel truly valued, they don't just show up—they invest themselves. That's leadership. That's transformation. And that's exactly what Austin Muchemore built.

When I left that day, after talking with Melissa, I wasn't thinking about percentages or metrics. I was thinking about what happens when a leader takes something good and makes it even better. Austin didn't just manage Hollywood Casino in Bangor—he elevated it. And that's the kind of leadership that creates a lasting impact.

Shelby: A Personal Declaration

Sometimes, declarations don't come with fanfare. They're not shouted from rooftops or posted in curated Instagram grids. The real ones—the declarations that change you—usually start in quiet moments, when no one else is watching.

That's how Shelby Soucy made hers.

I met Shelby and her husband Brett the way you meet good people in small towns—by proximity and providence.

My wife Bre and I had just moved into our home in Glenburn, Maine. Bre was nine months pregnant at the time—nine, not figuratively, literally. We were navigating all the beautiful chaos that comes with preparing for a baby—new home, new routines, and that hum of "are we ready for this?"

And then—enter the Soucys.

They weren't just neighborly. They were divine intervention in flannel. They showed up without hesitation, barely knowing us, and helped in all the ways that matter. A dropped-off meal when we didn't even realize we hadn't eaten. A quick text that said, "need anything from town?" at the exact moment we did. They didn't overstep—they stepped *in*. Always kind. Always present. They were the kind of people who made us feel like maybe, just maybe, we were going to be okay.

We became friends fast. Over time, those firepit huddles and casual driveway check-ins turned into something deeper—conversations that moved past small talk and into real connection. We talked about parenting, marriage, business, and everything else under the sun.

They told me about Frank's Bakery—the family business they ran together in Bangor. I told them about my work as a leadership and development consultant. Before long, we were working together professionally too, digging into their team's growth, how to lead better, live better, and show up better. Our conversations always started friendly and ended the same way.

It was during one of those conversations that Shelby said something that had nothing to do with work, but everything to do with *purpose*.

She told me she was going to run a marathon.

Now, if you know Shelby, you know this wasn't some whimsical daydream or post-New Year's resolution. This was a declaration. A full-on, soul-level promise to herself. It was personal. It was bold. And it was real.

She didn't train with a group or hire a coach. She researched alone, pulling plans off *Runner's World* and other sites—comparing twelve-, fourteen-, sixteen-, and twenty-week programs until she found one that fit. No spotlight. No status update. Just Shelby, her schedule, her shoes, and the hilly back roads of small-town Maine.

Her gear? Two pairs of sneakers worn into the ground. A reflective vest that held her water and her mace. A Fitbit to track her stats. And that was it. No performance gear. No hype playlist. Just Shelby and the cold wind of early morning runs.

Every once in a while, I'd catch her out there—me driving, her pounding the pavement on the side of the road. I'd hit the horn, pump my fist in the air, or send her a *"you got this"* text afterward. I wasn't part of her plan—but I was darn proud to be part of her belief.

She told me there were two days that defined her journey. The first was when she genuinely believed she couldn't do it. The second was the day she *knew she could.*

"My body held up," she told me, reflecting on the journey. "It was my mind that had to make peace with my will."

That's the line. That's the shift. That's when a declaration becomes destiny.

Because this was never about running.

This was about *becoming.*

When she crossed that finish line, she wasn't just proving something to others. She was honoring every promise she made to herself. Every mile no one saw. Every early alarm she didn't snooze. Every moment she chose to keep going when she could've called it quits. That finish line was a mirror—reflecting a woman who followed through.

And she's not done.

This October, she'll take on the Maine Marathon again—the same course she conquered two years ago. Her training starts June 1, one week before she turns fifty-one.

And let me be clear—she's not running to prove she's *still got it*. She's running because she knows she *never lost it*.

This wasn't just about fitness.

This was a personal declaration—in the purest form.

What These Examples Teach Us

Both Austin and Shelby had one thing in common: they didn't just make declarations—*they lived them*. Their success wasn't luck. It was built on clear commitments, checkpoints to stay on track, and accountability to the right people.

Now it's your turn. *What's your Austin moment? When are you gonna boss up like Shelby?* What's the one declaration that's gonna light a fire under your team—or under your own self? Remember, the power of a declaration isn't in saying the words. It's in doing the work, building the habits, and surrounding yourself with people who'll push you to follow through.

Leadership Will Make You Bleed: Tackling Resistance Head-On

Let's not play—*declarations are terrifying.* You're putting yourself on the line. Staking your name, your credibility, and your reputation on something that hasn't even happened yet. And the fear of failing—*failing publicly*—is enough to make most people stay quiet, play small, and avoid the risk altogether.

And if your goal is to *never fail,* be honest with yourself—you're also making sure you *never grow.* Failure happens. It's how you respond that matters. Leadership can't be about avoiding risks. It's about stepping into risks, knowing full well that you'll take some hits. It will *test you.* It will *break you down.* And it will *leave its mark.* But that's the job. You make the hard calls. You carry the weight no one else will. You take responsibility when things go wrong and stand firm when the pressure is at its highest. Under those circumstances, make no mistake—leadership will make you bleed. Not just once, but over and over again.

I first heard the term "Bleeder-ship" at a leadership conference with Dr. Sam Chand at Faith Bible College International in Charleston, Maine. Sam is one of the most brilliant leadership minds of our time, and his insights that day cut straight to the heart of what it means to lead with sacrifice. His words stuck with me. "If you're not bleeding, you're not leading."

That phrase sat with me long after the session ended. I had the privilege of speaking with Sam afterward, and his wisdom reinforced something I've always believed: real leadership isn't just about making declarations—it's about bleeding for them. Putting it all on the line for your people.

As an emerging leader, *fear of* failure often shows up in specific ways. Maybe it's the *fear of* taking on a stretch project that could either boost your career or expose your inexperience. Maybe it's the *fear of* making a bold suggestion in a meeting with senior executives. Or maybe it's the *fear of* leading your first team and not living up to expectations.

These are all normal fears. And you can't let them define your leadership.

Struggle Isn't Failure—It's Proof You're Still in the Fight

Bethany Ordung, PE, a standout graduate of the HG Leadership Journey I facilitated at Haley Ward in 2024, said it best: "Struggling is not failing."

That simple phrase hit me harder than any participant's tagline ever had. Why? Because it's a mindset that changes everything—and one we can all benefit from.

Struggling often gets a bad rap, but let's reframe it. Struggling means you're willing to brawl for it. It's proof that you're pushing forward, confronting challenges, and doing the work that matters. Real failure only happens when you quit—when you stop trying altogether. So, if you're feeling that internal resistance creeping in, don't let it stop you. Instead, *use it as fuel*. Here are five practical tips to help you push through and stay committed to your declaration.

1. Start Small, but *Start*

If the thought of making a bold, public declaration feels overwhelming, don't jump straight to declaring a company-wide initiative. Start with something smaller and more focused. *For example,* declare to your direct team that you'll implement biweekly check-ins to improve communication. Or . . . commit to sharing one innovative idea in the next leadership meeting. These smaller wins build confidence and momentum, which you can leverage for larger declarations later.

2. Reframe Failure

In the corporate world, failure is often seen as a career-ending setback. But in reality, failure is one of the most powerful teachers you'll ever encounter. Leaders who fear failure also fear growth—because avoiding failure means avoiding the lessons that come with it. A popular quote often attributed to Nelson Mandela captures this well: "I never lose. I either win or learn." Regardless of who first said it, the truth remains—every misstep is an opportunity, not an endpoint.

That's the mindset of a true leader. Missing a goal or falling short on a declaration isn't the end—it's an opportunity to reflect, adapt, and come back stronger.

What defines your leadership isn't the fact that you failed; it's how you respond to it. Reframing failure starts by asking yourself: *What would I regret more—trying and failing, or never trying at all?* For most leaders, the regret of inaction lingers far longer than the sting of a stumble.

3. Focus on the Process, Not the Outcome

Declarations aren't just about achieving a single result—they're about who you become in the process. As a leader, the journey matters just as much as the destination. Instead of obsessing over the final outcome, focus on building the habits, skills, and relationships that will move you forward. *Did you create a plan? Did you communicate effectively with your team? Did you show resilience when things got tough?* Those are the markers of success.

4. Use Fear as Fuel

Fear isn't your enemy—it's your compass. If something scares you, it's probably worth doing. That presentation to senior leadership that makes your palms sweat? That's the kind of challenge that builds your credibility. The team decision that could backfire? That's how you gain trust by showing decisiveness.

5. Lean on Your Own *Square Squad*

Fear thrives in isolation. When you keep your declaration to yourself, you're left alone with the *what-ifs.* Share your declaration with your own squad—the trusted few who will hold you accountable and remind you why you started. They don't just cheer you on; they push you to keep going when it feels hard.

As a leader, fear isn't what holds you back—it's the way you respond to fear that grabs your ankles and trips you up. So, feel the fear, and go do it anyhow! Do it with a lump in your throat, do it with shaky hands or a trembling voice, do it with poop in your pants. (*Okay, maybe that's too far—but you get the point.*) But somehow, like the slogan on my Nikes . . . *Just do it!*

Practical Tools to Make Your Declarations Stick

Making a declaration is one thing—following through is another. To close the gap between *what you say* and *what you do*, you need tools. Practical, no-nonsense tools that keep you focused, accountable, and moving forward. Here are three game-changers to help you turn your declarations into results:

1. Declaration Worksheet

This isn't just a blank page—it's your roadmap. A Declaration Worksheet forces you to clarify your commitment, dig into your *why*, and establish a plan of action. Use these prompts to get started:

1. **What am I declaring?** (Get specific. No vague aspirations allowed.)
2. **Why is this important to me?** (Tie it to your values or long-term vision. This is your fuel.)
3. **Who will I share this with?** (Choose your own Square Squad—pick the right people to hold you accountable.)
4. **When will I check in on my progress?** (Set clear milestones to keep yourself on track.)

Fill it out, print it, and put it where you can see it every day. Because out of sight? Out of mind. (See the Sample Declaration Worksheet Template below).

Declaration Worksheet Template (Blank)

1. What am I declaring?

____

____

____

2. Why is this important to me?

____

____

____

3. Who will I share this with?

____

____

____

4. When will I check in on my progress?

____

____

____

5. What are the potential challenges, and how will I address them?

____

____

____

6. How will I celebrate success?

____

____

____

2. Declaration Calendar

Think of this as your declaration's GPS. The calendar maps out the milestones leading to your goal, so you know exactly where you stand at any given moment.

Here's how to set it up:

1. Break your declaration into specific, measurable checkpoints *(monthly, weekly, or even daily).*
2. Assign dates/times to each checkpoint, creating a clear timeline.
3. Build in flexibility for the unexpected—because life happens.

For example: If your declaration is to improve team productivity in six months, your calendar might include:

- Month 1: *Meet with the team to identify bottlenecks.*
- Month 2: *Implement a new project management tool.*
- Month 3: *Check in on adoption rates and adjust training as needed.*

This calendar isn't just for you—it's a tool to keep your team aligned and motivated. (See the Sample Declaration Calendar Template.)

Declaration Calendar Template (Sample)

Declaration: *"I will improve team communication by holding biweekly one-on-one meetings with each team member over the next three months and tracking key discussion points to measure progress."*

Timeline: Three months (January 1 – March 31).

Date	Milestone	Status/Notes
Week 1: Jan 2	Announce the plan to the team during the weekly meeting.	Share the *why* behind the initiative and set expectations.
Week 2: Jan 8	Schedule one-on-one meetings with each team member.	Ensure all team members have a meeting slot by this date.
Week 3-4: Jan 15-Jan 31	Hold the first round of one-on-one meetings.	Use prepared questions to assess individual concerns and goals.
Week 6: Feb 10	Reflect on initial feedback from team members about the process.	Gather input on meeting effectiveness and make adjustments.
Week 8: Feb 28	Conduct second round of one-on-one meetings.	Address any follow-ups from the first round.
Week 10: Mar 10	Check in with my squad or trusted partner for feedback on progress.	Evaluate if the initiative is improving communication as planned.
Week 12: Mar 31	Conduct third round of one-on-one meetings and evaluate overall success.	Compare initial concerns to final outcomes; share results with the team.
April 5: Bonus Milestone	Celebrate success with the team.	Host a lunch or recognition event to acknowledge progress.

Blank Declaration Calendar Template

Declaration: [Write your specific declaration here.]
Timeline: [Specify your timeline here, e.g., three months, six months.]

Date	Milestone	Status/Notes
Week 1:	[Describe your first step or action item.]	[Leave space to track your status and notes.]
Week 2:	[Outline the next key milestone.]	
Week 3-4:	[Describe a recurring or ongoing task.]	
Week X:	[Include mid-point reflection or progress check-in.]	
Week X:	[Describe subsequent steps or adjustments.]	
Final Week:	[Outline the final step or milestone.]	
Post Timeline:	[Include a celebration or review milestone, if applicable.]	

Declaration:

Timeline:

Date	Milestone	Status/Notes
Week 1:		
Week 2:		
Week 3-4:		
Week X:		
Week X:		
Final Week:		
Post Timeline:		

3. Accountability Contracts

Sometimes, saying it isn't enough—you need to put it *in writing*. An Accountability Contract formalizes your commitment and makes it real. Think of it as a handshake agreement with your squad or your trusted partner.

Here's what to include in your contract:

- **Your Declaration:** Clearly state what you're committing to.
- **Timeline:** Specify when each milestone will be completed.
- **Support Plan:** Outline how your accountability partner *(or group)* will check in with you (weekly calls, monthly updates, etc.).
- **Consequences and Rewards:** Add stakes to the game. For example, *"If I miss the deadline, I'll donate $100 to a charity of my accountability partner's choice. But, if I hit the goal, we'll use that same $100 to celebrate with dinner."*

By writing it down and sharing it, you're taking your declaration to the next level. You're not just hoping for success—you're ensuring it.

Accountability Contract (Sample)

Declaration: *"I will improve team communication by holding biweekly one-on-one meetings with each team member over the next three months and tracking key discussion points to measure progress."*

Contract Terms:

1. Accountability Partner(s):
    - Name(s): [Trusted colleague, squad member, or team lead]
    - Role: Provide feedback, check in on progress, and hold me accountable to my timeline.

2. Commitments:
    - My Commitment:
        - Schedule and hold biweekly one-on-one meetings with all team members.
        - Collect feedback after each round of meetings and make necessary adjustments.
        - Share progress with my accountability partner at key checkpoints.
    - Partner's Commitment:
        - Ask for updates biweekly on progress.
        - Provide honest feedback on whether the meetings are achieving their intended goals.
        - Offer support or solutions if I encounter obstacles.

3. Milestones and Check-Ins:
    - *Week 1:* Share the plan with the team and schedule meetings.
    - *Week 3:* Complete the first round of one-on-one meetings and review outcomes with my partner.

- *Week 6:* Gather mid-point feedback and make necessary adjustments.
- *Week 12:* Complete the initiative, evaluate overall success, and share results.

4. Consequences and Rewards:

- If I follow through: Celebrate success with my team and host a recognition lunch.
- If I fall short: Write a personal reflection on what held me back and share it openly with my accountability partner.

5. Agreement:

By signing this agreement, I commit to following through on my declaration and maintaining open communication with my accountability partner throughout the process.

Signature (Declarer):

____

Date: ________________________

Signature (Trusted Partner):

____

Date: ________________________

Accountability Contract Template (Blank)

Declaration:

[Write your specific declaration here.]

____

____

____

Contract Terms:

1. Accountability Partner(s):
    - Name(s):

      ____

      ____

      ____

    - Role:

      ____

      ____

      ____

2. Commitments:
    - My Commitment:
        - [Write your specific actions or responsibilities.]

      ____

      ____

      ____

    - Partner's Commitment:
        - [Describe how they will support you and hold you accountable.]

      ____

      ____

      ____

3. Milestones and Check-Ins:
   - [Include specific dates and actions for progress updates.]

     ____

     ____

     ____

4. Consequences and Rewards:
   - If I follow through:
     - [Describe how success will be celebrated.]

     ____

     ____

     ____

   - If I fall short:
     - [Outline consequences for missing commitments.]

     ____

     ____

     ____

5. Agreement:

By signing this agreement, I commit to following through on my declaration and maintaining open communication with my accountability partner throughout the process.

Signature (Declarer):

____

Date: ________________

Signature (Partner):

____

Date: ________________

The Bottom Line

Tools don't do the work for you, but they help make the work clear, increasing the likelihood that it actually gets done. They give you structure, precision, and accountability—the things every leader needs to stay the course. So, grab the worksheet, map out your timeline, and lock in your accountability contract. Because declarations don't succeed on intention alone—they succeed with action.

Declarations Are Only as Strong as Their Execution

Declarations are powerful. Failure to execute them is the only thing more powerful. When a leader fails to honor their declaration, the fallout is significant. A declaration left unfulfilled isn't just a missed goal; it's a *breach of trust.*

As a leadership consultant, I've seen this ripple effect far too often: team members feel disappointed and disheartened, performance and morale decline, and the leader's credibility takes a major hit. Hard truth? In the MADE system, a failed declaration is worse than no declaration at all. Why? Because it doesn't just stall progress—it chips away at the trust your team depends on.

And just so we're clear—a *declaration* that isn't met didn't fail. The *execution* did.

The words were right. The follow-through wasn't. The declaration itself remains valid, powerful, and valuable. But when execution falters, trust erodes. Leaders who declare a commitment and don't follow through aren't just disappointing their teams—they're actively undermining their own leadership and their team's confidence in them.

To ensure your declarations lead to success, execution must be treated as a separate, deliberate step. It's not enough to simply mean well; you need the right tools, a clear plan, and a relentless focus on action. The resources we've discussed—like declaration worksheets, declaration calendars, and accountability contracts—aren't just helpful; they're essential. They are the infrastructure that bridges the gap between *intention* and *action*. Without them, even the boldest declaration risks falling flat.

But what does this look like in practice? Before we dive into *Execution*—the final and arguably most critical step of MADE—we'll explore a real-world case study of a leader who made a bold declaration. You'll see what went right, where things went off track, and how they navigated the challenges of follow-through. This example will bring everything we've discussed to life and set the stage for understanding how execution transforms declarations into tangible outcomes.

Case Study: A Bold Declaration at St. Croix Tissue, Inc.

The tension in the room was palpable.

Maintenance and Operations, two critical teams at St. Croix Tissue, Inc. (SCT), sat on opposite sides of the table, divided not just by roles but by years of miscommunication and frustration. Both teams were essential to SCT's success, yet their inability to collaborate was creating ripple effects across the organization. Communication was inconsistent, accountability was unclear, and frustrations were mounting. This discord wasn't just affecting morale—it was starting to impact productivity.

St. Croix Tissue, Inc., based in Baileyville, Maine, is a leader in innovative tissue manufacturing, known for its cutting-edge technology and commitment to sustainability. With its state-of-the-art facilities and focus on employee development, SCT had always set the standard for excellence. But even the most forward-thinking companies face internal challenges, and this was a big one.

Dan Ludden, SCT's Mill Manager, recognized the urgency of the situation. With the support of Vice President Marty Richard, Dan brought me in to work with their key leadership teams. The goal was clear: repair the rift between Maintenance and Operations, improve accountability, and rebuild trust.

During our very first leadership session, Dan didn't just make a statement—he made a bold, uncompromising declaration:

"Within six months, we will transform how Maintenance and Operations communicate, collaborate, and hold each other accountable. Together, we will build a stronger, more unified team."

He delivered this with fire in his voice and conviction in his eyes, before I even had a chance to speak. As he introduced me to the two teams, his heart took over, and he went off on a passionate tangent. I scrambled to jot down every word, knowing his energy could set the tone for what we were about to accomplish.

I was only there to lead an *Assertive Communication & Conflict Management* seminar that day, but Dan had just redefined the stakes. This wasn't just about communication anymore—this was about transformation. He had thrown down the gauntlet with his declaration, and in that moment,

I decided I would do everything in my power to make his vision a reality.

Dan's declaration wasn't just about resolving a temporary conflict—it was about fostering a culture of empathy, respect, and shared goals. With Marty's backing, the declaration became a company-wide initiative, signaling to everyone that collaboration and accountability were essential to SCT's success.

Dan identified three priorities for the initiative:

1. Establish clear, effective communication channels between Maintenance and Operations.
2. Create empathy between the teams by helping them understand each other's challenges and perspectives.
3. Develop accountability systems to ensure smoother collaboration during high-pressure situations, such as Shut Down Days.

This initiative was guided by the MADE framework, which allowed the teams to work through each phase of the process—from understanding the root issues to making and executing their own declarations.

What Went Right

From the outset, SCT leadership demonstrated their commitment to making this declaration a success:

1. **Leadership Workshops**
   We conducted workshops with leaders from both Maintenance and Operations, focusing on candid discussions about pain points and solutions. One of the major breakthroughs came when team members shared their frustrations openly in smaller breakout sessions, a

format that encouraged participation from those hesitant to speak up in larger groups.

2. **Team-Wide Declarations**
   To drive home accountability and shared responsibility, every member of both teams made a personal declaration to their teammates. Each person committed to at least one area they would improve to make their best contribution to the team. Just as importantly, they shared how their teammates could best hold them accountable. As Dan put it: "This process wasn't just about improving communication—it was about *redefining how we work together*. It's made all the difference." These declarations ensured that execution wasn't just Dan's responsibility—it belonged to everyone.

3. **Empathy Exercises**
   A key breakthrough came through building empathy between the two teams. I led targeted conversations and hands-on activities that helped them step into each other's world. Maintenance began to grasp the intense pressure Operations faced to hit production deadlines. And Operations finally saw the uphill battle Maintenance fought during unexpected breakdowns—with limited resources and even less time. That mutual understanding didn't just improve communication—it became the turning point in rebuilding trust.

4. **Structured Communication**
   Weekly cross-departmental check-ins were introduced, creating a consistent platform for updates and problem-

solving. Leaders from both teams co-led these meetings, reinforcing collaboration.

5. **Leadership Support**
   Marty Richard played a pivotal role in reinforcing the declaration's importance. His visible involvement signaled that this wasn't just an Operations issue—it was a top priority for SCT's success.

Challenges Along the Way

Transforming team dynamics is never smooth, and SCT encountered its share of setbacks. One significant hurdle was encouraging team members to speak up in larger group settings. Many felt intimidated or hesitant, which initially slowed progress. Smaller breakout discussions and 1:1's helped build confidence, but it required time and effort to bring everyone to the table.

The most critical challenge came during a Shut Down Day, a high-pressure period when both teams needed to work seamlessly to execute planned maintenance. Tensions flared, tempers ran high, and communication broke down.

Dan and Marty stepped in decisively, calming the situation and using it as a *teachable moment.* They reminded the teams of their shared goals, facilitated a resolution, and recommitted to the declaration. This moment of reflection and accountability reinforced their commitment to the process.

The Results

By the end of six months, the results were undeniable:

Improved Communication: Weekly check-ins and structured updates became a standard practice, reducing misunderstandings and increasing transparency.

Stronger Collaboration: Empathy exercises led to a significant shift in how the teams interacted, fostering greater respect and mutual support.

Enhanced Accountability: Team-wide declarations created a culture of shared responsibility, with every member actively contributing to the initiative's success.

Positive Morale: Participant engagement surveys showed a 30 percent improvement in inter-departmental relationships, with team members expressing greater satisfaction in how they worked together.

While not every team member made it through the process—some chose to leave, *but not all turnover is bad turnover*—those who stayed witnessed a remarkable transformation. SCT has become a healthier, more collaborative workplace.

One key employee in fostering empathy between the two groups, Chad James, a Project Engineer, summed it up perfectly:

"We're not just working better—we're working 'together' better."

Today, the practices established during this initiative remain embedded in SCT's culture, serving as a foundation for continued success. Collaboration and accountability are no longer just ideals—they are cornerstones of how SCT's teams operate every day.

Key Takeaways

St. Croix Tissue's journey highlights several lessons for all leaders:

- Empathy is a Game-Changer: Understanding each other's challenges fosters trust and collaboration.
- Accountability is Everyone's Responsibility: By involving every team member in the declaration process, SCT created a culture where execution wasn't just top-down—it was shared.
- Leadership Sets the Tone: Dan's bold declaration and Marty's unwavering support ensured the initiative stayed on track.
- Setbacks Are Opportunities: SCT turned high-pressure moments into learning experiences, strengthening their teams in the process.

St. Croix Tissue's story isn't just about solving a problem—it's about building a foundation for lasting success. With their new culture of accountability and collaboration, SCT is well-positioned to tackle future challenges and continue leading the tissue industry.

The Courage to Follow Through and Sink It

You now understand that a MADE style declaration isn't just words—it's a promise, a commitment that carries real weight.

But *declarations mean nothing without the courage to follow through*. The best leaders don't just make promises—they keep them. They understand that an unkept promise is a trust broken, a dream deferred, and a legacy lost.

This is your moment of truth. Ask yourself: "What am I willing to declare today? What commitments will I make, not just to myself, but to those counting on me to show up?" And then decide: Will you execute? Will you actually do the work to make it real?

Execution is where real leaders are forged. It's where intentions are measured, grit is tested, and discipline is proven. No one succeeds just because they have a perfect plan, but everyone who succeeds does so with relentless persistence.

This is your call to action. *Are you ready to step into the discomfort of growth, to silence excuses, and to turn your dreams into discipline?* This is the moment to stop rehearsing and start performing. Where you rise above the noise, leave the comfort zone behind, and face the climb with everything you've got.

The path to greatness is steep, uneven, and unforgiving—but it's yours to walk. Greatness isn't about reaching the top unscathed; it's about showing up every day, battered, bleeding, and bruised but still climbing. There's no magic, no shortcut—just your willingness to do the work.

So, what will it be?

Talk or action?

Excuses or effort?

Sinking or swimming?

I'd say it's time to declare it. Do it. Call your shot.

Because in the next chapter, we're going to make darn sure that when you take your shot—*you sink it*—exactly the way you said you would! It's time to Execute.

9

Execution – The Real Test of Leadership

Declarations are bold. They're the spark that ignites the fire, the words that claim your commitment. But let's not sugarcoat this—words are cheap. Anyone can declare their intentions, post their goals, and talk a big game. Execution is where the truth shows up. It's the battlefield where dreams are tested, where intentions face the grind of effort, and where you find out if you have the guts to follow through.

So, this is your moment of truth. Execution doesn't care about your excuses, your comfort zone, or how badly you want something. It only cares about what you're willing to do. It demands sweat, resilience, and showing up when it's inconvenient, exhausting, or downright painful. Declarations may inspire you (and others), but execution defines you (to others). It's where promises are made real—or broken.

Think about National Quit Day—that infamous day in January when millions of people, statistically speaking, are most likely to abandon their New Year's resolutions. They start the year with good intentions, but by the second Friday of January (Quitter's Day), they've already stopped showing up. Why? Because resolution without execution is just a wish. That's the difference between those who quit and those who succeed. True leaders don't celebrate the promise; they celebrate the follow-through. They show up when others don't and prove their declarations every single day.

Execution is the grind. It's where your declaration stops being a dream and starts becoming a legacy. This isn't just the final step of the MADE system—it's the culmination of everything you've been building toward. This is where you find out if you're serious. No shortcuts, no applause, no guarantees—it's just the work. So, I'll ask you one more time: Are you ready to prove it? Because execution doesn't wait. It's go time!

The Anatomy of Execution: What It Takes

Your declaration defined your why. Execution defines your how. This is where promises, plans, and good intentions either turn into results or die as just another unrealized idea. Execution is the great separator—it's what distinguishes dreamers from doers.

There is a reason that the leap from declaration to execution is where most people stumble. Declarations feel exciting—they're packed with energy and hope. But execution? Execution is just straight-up work. That's it. That's all. And it's often repetitive, inconvenient, and anything but glamorous. Yet without it, your declaration is just noise—empty words that lead nowhere.

So how do you make sure you show up and do the work? It boils down to three things: consistency, adaptability, and discipline. They're important, so let's break these down.

Consistency: The Power of Showing Up

Consistency is king. It's not about doing something perfectly—it's about doing it regularly. Progress isn't made in occasional bursts of inspiration; it's forged in the steady grind of consistent effort.

Over the course of a month, you'll spend about an hour brushing your teeth—one minute after your morning coffee and another after your last meal. Two tiny daily actions that keep your smile healthy and white.

But what if you brushed for sixty straight minutes on the first day of the month—and skipped the rest? Same amount of time, right? But we both know you'd still be headed for cavities—and breath hotter than those dragons on Game of Thrones.

In leadership, it's no different. Small, steady actions build results. The leader who checks in with their team for five minutes daily will foster trust that no quarterly meeting or one-time email blast can match. Execution isn't about heroic efforts; it's about showing up, doing the work, and letting the results stack over time. Again, small, steady actions build results.

Whatever you do all the time, that's who you are. It's that simple. Your habits define you. If you don't like who you are or where your life is headed, take a hard look at what you do day in and day out. Are you playing video games for hours or scrolling endlessly on your phone? Are you shopping for things you don't need? Are you watching people you barely know live their lives while you ignore your own?

If that's how you spend your time, then that's who you are. Change starts when you stop hiding behind distractions and start building a life that actually reflects who you want to be.

But if you want to be something different—a reader, a creator, a leader—it starts with what you consistently choose to do. The key word there is choose . . . it's your choice. But you can't keep living the same way and expect different results. That's insanity.

Maybe it's gaming. Maybe it's mindlessly scrolling on your iPhone. Or maybe it's something else entirely. Procrastinating. Complaining. Overanalyzing. Doubting yourself into inaction. Whatever it is—you know what it is.

But what if you repurposed that time to something constructive? Could you be investing the time you waste gaming or mindlessly scrolling into reading, learning, or building something meaningful?

And I'm not saying gaming or scrolling is all bad. As pastimes, they're totally fine. But when they become habits—they own you. (And deep down you know it's true.)

And make no mistake, they're not just costing you time.

They're stealing your potential.

They're draining your productivity.

They're robbing your future legacy.

As Tony Robbins famously said, "It's not what we do once in a while that shapes our lives, but what we do consistently." MADE leaders know this truth: consistency isn't just a habit—it's the engine that drives every success story. Think about it. The people you admire—the leaders, the achievers, the game-changers—they didn't stumble into greatness. They made intentional choices, over and over, to build the life they wanted.

What are your choices saying about you?

Adaptability: Flex, Don't Fold!

Life will wreck your plans. That's a guarantee. Adaptability is the ability to recalibrate without quitting. Great leaders don't sink the ship when the first approach fails—they adjust the sails and keep going.

If your plan to hit the gym every morning falls apart because your boss shifts your work schedule last minute, don't quit—pivot. Try evenings. Try home workouts. No weights? No problem. All you need is approximately six feet of hard floor for push-ups, sit-ups, planks, and air squats. Trust me, those four alone can leave you sore enough to question your life choices. The goal stays the same, only the method changes.

It's easy to make excuses when we give in to the temptation of comfort and ease. I remember making my own—telling myself that since I didn't own a treadmill, Maine's brutal winters made it impossible to do my cardio workouts. (Impossible … That's what I'd told myself.)

Previously, I'd been in a good rhythm of running/walking three to eight miles nearly every morning during the fall months. Then, ten-degree weather hit, and my "good habit" froze just like the Maine terrain. What did I do? Unfortunately, for more than a month, I let the couch win.

But one day, while sitting on that couch, I picked up Nelson Mandela's masterpiece autobiography, *Long Walk to Freedom*. In it, he described being dirt poor and confined to a prison cell smaller than my bathroom. He, too, was a runner—except he was imprisoned. He couldn't leave. He had no freedom to run outdoors. So, what did he do? He adapted.

He ran in-place for forty-five minutes.

Then came 100 fingertip push-ups.

200 sit-ups.

50 deep knee-bends.

50 burpees.

A full-body grind—in the tightest of spaces.

Every. Single. Day.

Going nowhere but achieving so much.

That hit me hard. Neither iron bars nor armed guards impeded me, only a little cold weather. In reality, I had freedom. And I could even afford tools like a treadmill or an elliptical if I wanted one—yet there I was sitting on the couch, imprisoned by my own excuses.

In a moment of guilt and contemplation, I thought of *Madiba* (Nelson Mandela's revered clan name, often used as a term of respect and affection). Then, I closed the book, kicked off my privileged Ugg slippers, and started jogging in-place. The whole time, I thought about what it must've been like to do this in a Cape Town prison cell, with no freedoms aside from what warders (prison guards) who hated me were willing to offer.

Madiba's mindset motivated me.

That first night, it took me twelve minutes, but I managed a mile. The next night, two miles. By the end of the week, after my wife and kids had gone to bed, I was lacing up my New Balances and wearing a noticeable spot into the living room carpet. My max? Six miles—all tracked on my Apple Watch—and all earned in just three feet of space in my living room.

I was learning to adapt.

Too many people throw in the towel when their first plan falls apart, when things are no longer easy. Great leaders like Mandela know better. Great leaders pivot. They use what they have, even when they don't have much.

Because while the path might twist and turn, the destination doesn't change.

Discipline: Doing the Work Anyway

Don't confuse enthusiasm with motivation. Enthusiasm is a fraud—it shows up loud and proud when things feel easy but vanishes the moment the grind gets real. That's why the best leaders don't count on fleeting feelings to carry them. They lean on discipline.

Observe the contrast: the word enthusiasm comes from the Greek *enthousiasmos*, meaning "possessed by a god." It's the kind of energy that feels divine, almost otherworldly—until reality kicks in and it fades faster than a spark in a storm. Enthusiasm might get you started, but it won't carry you through the hard, repetitive work that real progress demands.

Discipline, on the other hand, comes from the Latin *disciplina*, meaning "instruction" or "teaching." It's about mastery, not magic. Discipline isn't flashy or fleeting—it's the steady hand guiding you when enthusiasm has long since disappeared.

Solid leaders understand this: feelings might spark the fire, but discipline keeps it burning. Feelings don't finish the work or shape you into something better—discipline does. It's having the grit to repeat a process, no matter how mundane, no matter how simple.

You've heard "practice makes perfect"?

Who do you think made the best pots—students told to make as many as they could, or students told to make just one perfect one?

Back in the 1980s, a professor at the University of Florida ran this exact experiment in his ceramics class. He split the students into two groups. One group was graded entirely on how many pots they made—the more, the better. The other was graded on a single piece: one perfect pot.

By the end of the semester, the best pots—by far—came from the quantity group. While the "quality" group was stuck in their heads—planning, theorizing, overthinking—the "quantity" group was doing reps. Failing forward. Learning. Adjusting. Improving.

They didn't wait for perfection.

They executed.

That's what discipline looks like. And that's how growth actually happens.

Execution Is Where Success Lives

Execution isn't always sexy. It's not about flashy presentations or Insta-worthy moments. It's about grinding it out in the unglamorous middle, day after day. Every leader you admire, every business you respect, every big goal you envy—they all happened because someone showed up and executed, not just once, but over and over again.

So how do you start? Small.

Don't get bogged down by the size of the vision—focus on what needs to be done today. Then, do it again tomorrow. The magic of execution lies in its momentum, in the way small wins build into big outcomes.

At the end of the day, execution is the difference-maker. It's the only way: Show up. Adapt. Execute. Every single day.

If you're ready to stop talking about success and start building it, it's time to get specific.

Execution isn't just about effort—it's also about intentionality and having a framework that makes action possible. Successful leaders don't rely on luck or motivation: They rely on a process. So, how do you move from lofty goals to tangible results? Let's check out the framework that will get you there.

The Execution Framework

Execution can't be 100 percent grit—it's also about having a plan. Declarations are exciting, but they're also incomplete. If you stop there, you're left with lofty assertions and no map to get you to the summit. MADE leaders don't leave their success up to chance; they break it down, build habits, and track their progress every step of the way. Here's the framework that turns your good intentions into the real results you desire:

1. Break It Down

Big goals are overwhelming, and that's why most people give up before they even start. The secret? Break it down into small, actionable steps that you can actually tackle. When you chunk the big picture into bite-sized pieces, progress transitions from possible—to inevitable.

Let's say you want to be like Shelby from earlier, and your declaration is, "I want to run a marathon." That sounds great in theory, but it's useless without a plan. Instead, make it specific:

"This week, I'll run three miles, four days of the week." That's a clear, manageable step. And once you conquer that, you build from there, and like Shelby you'll break down that barrier and cross the marathon finish line in due time. Great leaders know the key to big wins is starting small.

2. Establish Daily Habits

Consistency beats intensity every time. The best way to guarantee you'll show up day after day is to create habits that are automatic, repeatable, and non-negotiable.

Charles Duhigg, in his groundbreaking book *The Power of Habit*, explains the "habit loop"—a simple formula to understand and build lasting habits: Cue—Routine—Reward.

The cue is the trigger that reminds you to take action, like laying out your running clothes and shoes the night before.

The routine is the action itself—lacing up and hitting the pavement first thing.

The reward is what reinforces the habit, like the sense of accomplishment you feel after finishing the run.

And non-negotiables are your secret weapon. These are the actions you commit to no matter what. Too tired? Too busy? Doesn't matter—you do them anyway. Why? Because habits build momentum, and momentum builds success.

3. Build a System

Discipline is essential, but truthfully—depending on sheer willpower is a losing strategy. Successful leaders understand this. They don't gamble on willpower; they build systems that make execution easier and more sustainable.

A system could be as simple as a checklist or as robust as a productivity app. Use tools to keep yourself on track, whether it's a physical calendar, a digital task manager, or an accountability partner who's not afraid to call you out on your BS.

The beauty of systems is simple: they kill the guesswork. When structure is in place, you don't waste energy deciding what to do next—it's already decided. That's the power of discipline on autopilot.

And I don't care what anybody says—Tom Brady is the G.O.A.T. Back when he was still playing in the NFL, he didn't just rely on talent; he relied on systems. The man could tell you in the preseason what he was having for dinner on Thursday of Week 14. His TB12 Method laid it all out—what to eat, how much to eat, and when to eat it—all designed to keep his body in peak condition when it mattered most. He wasn't negotiating with cravings or scrolling through takeout menus. The system made the decision for him—so he could focus on winning. (And he did a lot of that.)

As James Clear wrote, "You don't rise to the level of your goals; you fall to the level of your systems." Brady didn't just set big goals—he built a system that backed them up. That's the real game: not hoping you'll rise to the occasion, but knowing your system won't let you fall.

4. Track Progress

Attributed to the great management guru Peter Drucker is a phrase I love: "What gets measured gets managed." Tracking your progress isn't just about staying accountable—it's about celebrating your wins and course-correcting when things go off track.

Set up regular check-ins, whether it's weekly, bi-weekly, or monthly. Use this time to ask yourself:

- *What worked?*
- *What didn't?*
- *What adjustments do I need to make?*

Using our previous example, if your goal is still to run three miles four times a week, check in every Sunday to see how you did. Did you hit your target? Great—celebrate that. If not, figure out why and adjust. Maybe you need to move your runs to a different time of day or add an accountability partner.

Tracking isn't about perfection; it's about progress. Solid leaders know that even small wins matter. When you acknowledge them, you build the confidence to keep going.

Ben Franklin notably said, "If you fail to plan, you plan to fail." Because execution doesn't happen by accident—it happens because you make it happen. Break it down. Build habits. Create systems. Track your progress. Then, do it all, again and again and again. Don't just hope and wish that you'll succeed—plan for it and then follow through.

And watch out for resistance, because you can be sure that it is lurking around the corner!

10

Execution – Tackling Resistance

Right now, as I write this, it's 5:08 AM on February 27. I'm sitting at my desk, staring at the blinking cursor, fighting off the fog of sleepiness. I admit, my grogginess and the freezing temps have me wrapped in a blanket and completely hunched over my keyboard. (If Breanne saw my posture right now, she'd certainly razz me to quit hunching and sit up straight.)

But curled forward, I opened the MS Word file that stores my book outline to see what today's writing will include, and wouldn't you know it? Today's topic: Tackling Resistance. The irony isn't lost on me—I'm living it right now.

No cap . . . getting out of bed this morning felt next to impossible. Every part of me begged to stay under the covers—warm, still, and inches away from the comforting smell of my wife's hair. My brain started hemorrhaging excuses like a dude trying to talk his way out of a speeding ticket. The self-talk was loud:

"You've earned a day to sleep in, TJ."

"You'll write better when you're not so tired, bro."

"C'mon, man—this doesn't really matter at 5 AM, does it? Most people don't even start 'til 8 o'clock."

But here I am—5:08 in the morning—showing up anyway. Because I've learned something: resistance feeds on those kinds of excuses. It doesn't come at you loud and cocky; it nudges. It whispers—just enough to make quitting sound reasonable.

What Resistance Looks Like In Action

Solid leaders execute even when it's hard—and especially when resistance tries to stop them. But resistance is most successful when it's sneaky. That's why it doesn't always show up as outright defiance. You'd recognize defiance, be irritated and challenged by it. Your competitive spirit would take over . . . and you wouldn't let it win.

So, resistance, like every villain revealed at the end of a Scooby-Doo episode, *disguises itself.* In the beginning, it appears as something harmless—or worse, practical:

- **Procrastination:** "I'll start tomorrow" (That one is the anthem of resistance.)
- **Distractions:** Checking your email, scrolling Facebook, or suddenly deciding the garage needs reorganizing.
- **Self-Doubt:** "Why bother? I'll probably fail anyway."

  In the declaration phase, resistance was mostly *internal*—fear of failure or hesitation to commit. But now, in *execution,* it shifts. Resistance starts throwing *external* barriers your way: packed schedules, unexpected setbacks, or competing priorities.

But effective leaders don't just overcome resistance—*they use it*, putting these external barriers to work for themselves. They know every challenge has something to teach, and every win, no matter how small, fuels momentum.

- **Reframe Challenges**
  Resistance isn't the enemy; it's your training ground. Successful leaders flip the script and see obstacles as chances to grow.

  Examples: Stuck in traffic and late for your gym session? Use the time to visualize your next workout plan. *Facing time constraints?* It's an opportunity to sharpen your prioritization skills. Resistance isn't stopping you—it's shaping you into someone stronger.

- **Use Micro-Wins**
  When the big picture feels overwhelming, focus on the next small step. Micro-wins are resistance's kryptonite—they make progress feel achievable and keep you moving forward.

  Example: Struggling to write a 10-page report? Just draft the first sentence. The victory of starting builds momentum for what's next. As Tommy Baker outlines in *The 1% Rule*, small wins stacked consistently lead to big results. Focus on progress, not perfection—and the big wins will take care of themselves.

- **Accountability**
  Resistance hates accountability. Sharing your goals with someone who won't coddle your excuses forces you to show up—even when you don't feel like it.

Example: Pair up with a no-BS accountability partner. They're not there to cheerlead; they're there to make sure you follow through. Knowing you have to answer to someone can be the push you need to fight through the toughest resistance.

A High-Flying Flagg: Lessons in Relentless Discipline

You don't need to be perfect to win—you just need to be persistent. The best executors aren't flawless; they're disciplined and consistent. They might miss a day, but they never miss two.

Take Cooper Flagg, the basketball phenom from Newport, Maine. He made national waves with his stellar play at Duke University—in my birthplace of Durham, North Carolina—and was selected as the No. 1 overall pick in the 2025 NBA Draft by the Dallas Mavericks.

Flagg's meteoric rise wasn't built on talent alone. It was forged through relentless, consistent effort that started long before the spotlight found him.

Growing up, Flagg didn't just practice when the gym lights were on; he was still grinding long after everyone else went home. His mornings started early with drills to perfect his shot, and his nights often ended with film study, dissecting every detail of his game. Even as a teenager, his commitment to daily improvement was unmatched. Whether it was refining his footwork or dialing in his defensive intensity, Flagg focused on stacking small wins every day. He wasn't chasing perfection in one leap—he was building it brick by brick. That's how he became the player who now dominates the court with confidence and precision.

I'm fortunate to have shared a community with Flagg during his formative years, able to watch his development and witness parts of his progression. His principal trainer (one of the top basketball trainers in the country), Matt MacKenzie, runs Eastern Maine Sports Academy (EMSA) in Veazie, Maine, just minutes from my house. My son, Jace, played AAU basketball for Matt's program during middle school, and there were times we'd see Cooper and Matt locked in during 1-on-1 training sessions at the far end of the state-of-the-art facility. Even their training sessions were a spectacle. Kids—and some parents—would stick around just for the chance to catch a glimpse, maybe snap a picture with Cooper, or score an autograph. I wasn't above it either—I mean, this is a generational talent we're talking about here. I made sure to grab a photo with Cooper and, mid-pose, of course, tried to nudge him toward the University of North Carolina over Duke. (It didn't work, but I'm Tar Heel until I die.)

What's remarkable about Cooper's journey, as Matt shared with me during an interview, is that his development wasn't an accident.

"We started by addressing the small things," Matt explained. "Cooper had talent, but talent alone isn't enough. He needed to commit to recovery, hydration, sleep, and consistency in his routines. We worked together to build habits that he could sustain over time—habits that made him more predictable in his performance."

Matt described the process as incremental: setting small, realistic goals and hitting them day after day. "When we started tracking things like his made shots or his sleep patterns, it clicked for him. He realized how those tiny habits stacked up over time can create gargantuan results. And once it clicked, he became almost obsessive about it. That's when I knew he was starting to own his development."

Cooper doesn't just want to compete. He has to win. It's not optional for him. It's not a switch he flips or a mood he's in—it's in his DNA. It's who he is.

I thought back to my times watching Matt work with Cooper at EMSA, and to my times on the sideline during his high school and AAU games here in Maine, where the truth about his bright future became impossible to ignore. You could see it in the way Cooper moved, in the way he attacked every single moment like it mattered. And it wasn't just during the games. You knew, even without seeing it, that he was the same way at 6 AM workouts, in empty gyms, in those lonely hours when nobody's watching.

That fire? That's what separates the good from the great—what Jim Collins, author of Good to Great, might call the leap from competence to true excellence. It's the kind of intensity that doesn't fade with the crowd. It lives in the effort, in the grind, in the relentless commitment to excellence when there's no one around to clap for you.

Cooper has it in spades.

One detail Matt highlighted stuck with me: the image of Cooper's "two hands held high after every shot." Matt, known for his meticulous attention to detail and ability to unlock an athlete's full potential, shared how this came to light while reviewing footage from Cooper's Duke games in late December 2024. Cooper had flown Matt from Maine to Durham to help address a concern that had been eating at him.

"He told me, 'My three-point shot doesn't feel right. My release isn't as consistent as I want it to be, and my follow-through doesn't feel clean'," Matt explained.

Determined to pinpoint the issue, Matt dove into the game film. His trained eye caught a subtle inconsistency in Cooper's motion—a slight variation in his wrist angle at the top of his release that disrupted the shot's trajectory. "A clean follow-through is like the punctuation mark on a sentence," Matt said. "Without it, your shot lacks clarity and confidence."

Once Matt identified the issue and communicated it, Cooper didn't hesitate. He committed to being hyper-intentional about locking in his follow-through. And it wasn't just something he practiced—it carried over into the games. Matt told me that from that point on, every three-point shot ended with Cooper's two hands held high, locked in place for a split second as if to stamp the moment into muscle memory. Repeatable execution. Locked in.

When I saw how Matt and Cooper trained together, I was in the midst of writing this very chapter on execution, and I immediately knew their story would be a winning addition. Their process embodies the principles that MADE is built on. As a reader, you can take inspiration from both of them. Like Cooper, you can adopt the discipline of tracking your progress, refining your techniques, and committing to relentless execution. Like Matt, you can identify the small, incremental changes that drive sustained growth, both in yourself and in those you lead.

Matt MacKenzie and Cooper Flagg's story isn't just about basketball. It's a masterclass in the power of showing up. Whether you're working on your craft, building a business, or chasing a goal, the formula is the same: small, steady actions build unstoppable momentum. Consistency beats perfection every single time.

So, ask yourself: What's your version of two hands frozen high? What small, deliberate action can you take today—and every day—that will make the difference? Whether it's nailing a presentation, closing a sale, or creating art, success isn't built on one perfect move. It's built on the thousands of deliberate repetitions that no one else sees.

Discipline Is the Protein

Discipline isn't dessert. It's not a side dish or a snack either. It's the protein in your leadership meal. Bloody and rare. Raw if it has to be. Without it, motivation's just garnish—looks good but won't fill you.

Solid leaders don't chase motivation. They cook a whole power meal from scratch—and devour the full plate, swallowing grit, consistency, and discipline. Here's how you can do it:

1. Habit Stacking

When it comes to building habits that actually stick, James Clear's Atomic Habits is the G.O.A.T. He didn't invent the idea, but he made "habit stacking" famous—and for good reason. Habit stacking is simple: take something you already do on autopilot, and tack a new habit onto it. Drink coffee every morning? Cool. Stack a goal review or a stretch session right on top. No goal review, no stretch—no coffee. That cup becomes your reward, and discipline becomes automatic. You don't need more willpower. You need better wiring. Stack the habits, build the system, and let discipline do the work.

In June 2025, I started working with Josh Morse, Director of Employee Benefits Sales at Cross Insurance Agency. Great leader. Even better man. Sharp, respected, and carrying a heavy load. In our first session, I talked about how important it is for leaders to start their day with intention. I shared how journaling has been a game-changer for me—simple, consistent, grounding. Josh listened, nodded, and said, "I just don't have time to journal or prep for my day."

He had time. What he didn't have was a system.

So we started small: no phone in the morning until he wrote one intention in a notebook by his bed. Took thirty seconds. That's it. By week two, we added a three-minute planning session while the coffee brewed. Just enough to set the tone—no fluff, no overwhelm. Two weeks in, his mornings were dialed in. His mindset shifted. And his team felt the difference.

Intentional mornings lead intentional teams. He didn't find more time—he took command of it. Discipline didn't show up out of nowhere—he built it. One stack at a time.

2. Morning Routines

Start your day on purpose or get dragged by it—those are the options. Whether it's journaling, moving your body, or locking in your top priorities, a strong morning routine isn't a luxury—it's a launchpad. Forget perfect. This isn't about sunrise yoga and green juice (unless that's your thing). It's about owning your first hour, so the rest of the day doesn't own you.

Years ago, I worked with a senior leader at a Machias Savings Bank in Downeast Maine. Heart of gold, culture champion, and on the edge of burnout.

She told me, "I feel like I'm putting out fires all day—but I never get to what matters."

So I asked her, "What's the first thing you do in the morning?"

She said, "Check emails in bed or in the kitchen."

Boom. That was it. She was waking up to other people's priorities, not her own.

We made one change: no email until after coffee. Her first fifteen minutes became quiet time, a quick journal entry, and writing down her top three priorities for the day. That was it. Two weeks in, everything shifted. She had more focus, more patience, and her team felt it. She wasn't reacting to the day anymore—she was setting the tone.

Control your morning, control your momentum.

3. Track Your Wins

Track your progress or forget your progress. Use a calendar, a habit app, a sticky note—whatever works. Seeing your streak stack up builds momentum, especially when the grind feels dry.

The competitor in you? That's not the enemy—it's the fuel. Use it.

I've got 797 straight days of Italian on Duolingo. Not because I'm obsessed with the language. Because they flash that streak number right on the app icon. If they didn't? I'd have tapped out at day thirty.

But that little number? It dares me to keep going. It says, "Don't break it." So I don't.

Che figata!

Benissimo!

Molto bene!

11

Execution – Mindset Shifting

No one's posting selfies of themselves habit stacking, grinding through routines, or journaling their half-percent improvements. But that's the difference—the dreamers post; the doers grind. MADE leaders get that. Just like all motivation is self-motivation, all discipline is self-discipline. And let's be real: there's nothing glamorous about it.

I'm exhausted by the endless parade of one-liners and motivational mottos plastered across LinkedIn. Sure, they sound good, maybe even feel good for a moment, but let's be for real—cute quotes don't close the gap between *where you are* and *where you want to be.*

If you want to cross the finish line, know that *your* success will boil down to *your* consistency, *your* focus, and, most importantly, a shift in how *you* think. If you don't change how you think, you'll never change what you do.

Carol Dweck's research in *Mindset* underscores how a *fixed mindset*—where perfection feels like the only acceptable outcome—can paralyze action and leave us stuck. MADE leaders break free from this cycle by embracing a *growth mindset,* focusing instead on consistent progress.

Think about it: perfection is an illusion, a mirage we chase but never reach. Progress, on the other hand, is tangible and transformative. It's the extra call you made, the revised draft you completed, or the small pivot that turned a challenge into a win. MADE leaders understand that progress, not perfection, is what moves the needle. It's the backbone of execution.

When you're tempted to obsess over every little detail, stop and ask: "Did I make progress today?" If the answer is *yes*, you're doing what matters. Keep going!

Get Better, Not Right

This focus on progress ties directly to the principles of the growth mindset. Smart leaders know they don't need to get everything right; they just need to get better. *Here's how they do it:*

- Effort Over Perfection: They recognize that mastery isn't about getting it right the first time. It's about showing up, doing the work, and staying in the game long enough to see improved results.
- Opportunities in Challenges: The best leaders embrace obstacles as opportunities. Instead of retreating, they lean in, asking, *what can I learn from this?*
- Feedback as Fuel: Execution without reflection is just motion. Solid leaders actively seek feedback, using it as a compass to refine their approach and grow.
- Progress Beats Paralysis: Those in a fixed mindset freeze at the prospect of imperfection. Great leaders, by contrast, act. Even imperfect action moves them closer to their goals.

The MADE system—Motivation, Assessment, Declaration, Execution—is built to align with a growth mindset. And Execution is where all these elements converge. *Motivation* fuels the effort, *Assessment* provides clarity, and *Declaration* solidifies commitment. *Execution,* then, transforms it all into tangible results. So, don't wait for perfect conditions. Dive in, adjust, and grow stronger with every move.

Ask yourself: Do I aim for progress, or do I paralyze myself chasing perfection? Am I willing to see challenges as opportunities? Can I commit to learning from every failure?

The answers to these questions define whether you're stuck in neutral or ready to drive your leadership to the next level. So, feel that fear, then execute anyway. Again, it's not about being fearless; it's about letting your actions speak louder than your doubts. Every small step forward is proof that you're not just talking about growth—you're living it.

Choose *Get To* Over *Have To*

Dweck's work reminds us that mindset isn't just about how we view our abilities—it's about how we frame our actions. MADE leaders understand the power of *reframing* and embrace the shift from seeing obligations as *burdens* to viewing them as *opportunities*. They learn to replace *"I have to"* with *"I get to."*

This truth came alive for me through one of my favorite people in the world, Zavier Scott. Zavier isn't just a mentee; he's my Godson. We met years ago at The Rock Church in Bangor, Maine, but our first interaction wasn't a conversation—it was a moment that left an indelible mark on my heart. I first saw him on stage at church, wearing cut-off shorts exposing his tree trunk legs and a black T-shirt that read *"I Have Decided."* He was being baptized.

Few times in my life have I known for certain that God was speaking directly to me, but this was one of them.

I felt a deep, unmistakable and unshakable tug in my spirit. I knew I had to reach out to him before he left the church parking lot that Sunday. That feeling was corroborated when I glanced over at my wife and saw tears streaming down her face as the pastor sank Zavier into the waters of the baptismal pool. When he emerged, he wasn't just drenched—he was radiant.

I reached out to Zavier in the church vestibule and introduced myself, and from there, our connection grew beyond anything I could have anticipated. Watching him evolve—from that powerful moment of baptism to excelling on the football field and in life—has been one of the greatest privileges of my life. He's more than a mentee; he's family.

When Zavier transitioned from playing football at the University of Maine to the NFL with the Indianapolis Colts, I remember asking him early on, "How is work?" He chuckled, then paused, almost surprised by the word. Football had never felt like "work" to him. So many people say they're "living the dream"—but Zavier truly was. For him, every practice, every play, every moment on the field is a gift, and he embraces it with a level of gratitude and positivity that is contagious.

Over time, our conversations often turned to the grind of his day-to-day responsibilities, and I found myself saying things like, *"You have to* wake up early*, you have to* prepare*, you have to* keep pushing, man.*"*

One day, he stopped me mid-sentence and said, "No, TJ, I don't *have to . . .* I *get to*."

That simple correction stopped me in my tracks.

Here was this young football player, early in his NFL career, teaching me—*the leadership coach*—something profound about the leadership mindset. He wasn't just correcting my language—he was reminding me that the way we frame our responsibilities *changes everything*. His positivity, his gratitude, and his sheer drive shifted my perspective, not just about him—but for myself. It wasn't about *having to* train, practice, or stay disciplined—it was about *getting to* chase a dream that so few ever achieve.

Zavier has since moved on to a new quest, now playing for the Minnesota Vikings. It's another chapter in his incredible journey, and I know he'll approach it with the same mindset that has always set him apart. Whether he's on the field or navigating life's challenges, Zavier embodies what it means to say, *"I get to."* He doesn't just see the privilege in his opportunities—he lives it, and that inspires everyone around him.

"I get to" isn't just a mental trick. It's a way of reclaiming power and finding purpose in every challenge. Tasks that once felt burdensome—early mornings, long hours, endless preparation—transform into privileges when you realize they're your chance to grow stronger, sharper, and better. Execution stops being something to endure and becomes something to embrace.

And Zavier's phrase and mindset is at the heart of the MADE approach. It's a lesson in gratitude, resilience, and purpose—a reminder that leadership begins with the mindset we bring to the table. Zavier doesn't just play the game—*he gets to.*

You do, too.

Your "Get To" Moment

I didn't *have to* wake up early and write this section of the book—I *got to*. I had the privilege of sitting down, reflecting, and sharing something that I hope will impact your life the way Zavier impacted mine.

So, here's my challenge to you: *What can you reframe in your own life? What is one thing that feels like an obligation that you can shift into an opportunity?* It might be waking up early, tackling a tough project, or even having a difficult conversation. Take a moment to think about it. What would change if you stopped saying "I have to" and started saying "I get to"?

The power of this mindset shift is transformative. Like Zavier, you can take what feels like a burden and turn it into a privilege. You don't just have to endure life—you *get to* embrace it.

So, what will you choose to *get to* do today?

12

Execution – A Story of Grit, Hustle, and Heart

I'm drawn to the stories of people who started at the bottom, kept grinding, and became somebody in this beast of a world. And that's exactly why I had to include this next one. It's about a CEO I know personally—not someone who inherited a title, but someone who earned every inch of it. Built something real. Took something good and made it great.

Meet my favorite CEO.

Today, Larry Barker is the President and CEO of Machias Savings Bank.

When he took the reins, the bank had $950 million in assets. Under his leadership, it didn't just grow—it exploded, tripling in size to $2.6 billion. That's more than impressive. That's insane! That's the kind of growth that shakes up an industry, disrupts the status quo, and makes competitors nervous.

But let's be real clear—the number isn't what makes Larry Barker legendary. It's how he got there.

Larry shouldn't be here running a billion-dollar bank and leading a company that has reshaped the financial landscape of Maine.

He shouldn't be here … He just shouldn't be.

Larry built himself from scratch. No shortcuts. No handouts. No favors. Just work. Hard, relentless, punch-you-in-the-mouth-and-keep-moving work. And that's why he's my favorite CEO.

Because success stories are nice. But the ones that come from the mud? The ones where a man has to claw his way up, step by step, with nothing but his will and his work ethic? Those are the stories that change the game. The ones worth telling.

Larry Barker is the real deal. Not because of the title. Not because of the money. But because of the climb. And if his story doesn't shake you, you can't be shook.

Larry's story to becoming a MADE leader encapsulates all the challenges of execution so fully, that I'd like to end this section by looking at his journey in more depth. If you take anything from his story, let it be this:

You don't need permission to be MADE.

You don't need an easy road.

You don't need anyone to give you a shot.

You just need to bet on yourself—and never back down.

That's exactly what Larry did.

A Childhood of Instability, Fear, and Loss

Larry spent his childhood waiting for the other shoe to drop. It always did. And it never landed quietly.

His father came back from Vietnam, but he never completely made it home. He was a presence without substance, a shadow of a man moving through their tiny apartment in Bangor, Maine. There in body but gone in every other way that mattered. Not haunted—at least, not in the way war movies would have you believe a soldier come home would be—but *absent*.

By the time Larry was six, his parents' marriage had crumbled. His mother, desperate to rebuild, remarried—

hoping for stability, for relief, for a man who would stand beside her in the fight.

Instead, she got another ghost. A used car salesman with a golden tongue and an even bigger hunger for booze and gambling. He could sell anyone on anything—*except* responsibility. He went to work. He drank. He gambled. He paid rent (once in a while). But overall, he left Larry's mother to carry it *all*. She was the one making sure the lights stayed on, the one stretching food stamps as far as they could go, the one feeding those growing boys with next to nothing.

Larry didn't know, back then, just how much weight mom was carrying.

Kids don't think about unpaid bills or the fridge being half-empty. They don't see the way a mother stares at the checkbook late at night, whispering numbers under her breath, hoping they stretch further than they do. They don't hear the deep sigh before she swipes her card at the grocery store, praying it goes through.

They don't notice the math a mother does in her head *every single day*.

How to make twenty dollars last until next week.

How to make one chicken stretch for three meals.

How to make a kid's birthday feel special with only three bucks, half a box of Betty Crocker cake mix, and two borrowed eggs.

Looking back now, Larry sees the fight she never stopped fighting. And through it all, the instability never stopped. The new schools. The new homes attached to new landlords—all pounding on the door, demanding money that never seemed to be there.

Larry learned *three things* very early in life:

1. Don't get attached.

2. Don't get comfortable.
3. Don't expect anyone to stay.

By the time he was ten, he knew how to pack a bag without asking questions. By twelve, he could see trouble coming from around the corner. Because in Larry's world, being naïve didn't just hurt—it left scars.

Then came the accident, when everything changed again.

Larry was twelve years old. He wasn't with his little brother, PJ. Not anywhere near the ATV where everything went wrong. Larry wasn't there when PJ died. He didn't see the moment. But he will always remember the aftermath—the flashing lights cutting through a quiet stretch of road outside Machias, EMTs moving with controlled urgency, adults huddling in tight circles, the unmistakable stillness that told him everything he needed to know.

He didn't need anyone to explain. Before a single word reached him, he knew which side of life he was now standing on.

The funeral came fast. Too fast. A closed-up silence fell over the house afterward. No one talked about it—not out of neglect, but because they didn't know how. They thought not talking about it would protect him, but all it did was teach him to carry his grief alone.

That day Larry cried until he couldn't cry anymore. And then he did what Larry has always done. He survived.

The Move That Saved Him

Larry had stopped believing in stability.

It was a fairytale—something other kids had. Other kids that had fathers who stuck around. Other kids that lived in homes where the rent was paid on time. Other kids who didn't have to keep their bags half-packed, waiting for the next move.

But Larry had spent his whole childhood in motion, learning that nothing was permanent, that no place was home.

Until he reached Machias, Maine. A town of barely 2,000 people. No skyscrapers. No headlines. Just a small, unassuming dot on the map. But for Larry? It was everything. Because Machias gave him what he had never had before: *roots*.

It wasn't just the place. It was the people. His people.

His grandparents. The kind of grandparents every kid should have—warm, present, steady. The kind who kept the fridge stocked with orange juice and tubs of ice cream. The kind who never let a child doubt for a second that they were loved.

His two sets of aunts and uncles. Hardworking, grounded, rock-solid. The kind of people who modeled strength, responsibility, and what it meant to be good. They didn't just welcome him into their lives. They made him part of them. They opened their homes. They opened their hearts. And they never gave up on him.

But if one person changed everything for young Larry Barker—it was Uncle Bob.

Uncle Bob Carter wasn't just another relative. He was the first man in Larry's life who didn't let him down. And that changed everything for him.

Bob Carter was a businessman. A self-made man. The kind of guy who carried a quiet strength. He was the kind who looked you in the eye and made you feel like you mattered. And when Bob learned what Larry had been through—the father who was a ghost, the stepdad who was dead weight, the years of instability—he didn't offer sympathy. He offered himself.

Bob made it his business to show up for Larry. To be there.

When Bob said he'd take Larry fishing, *he was there.*

When Bob said he'd swing by the house, *he knocked on the door.*

When Bob said, "You can do it," he said it like *it was a fact, not a question.*

At first, Larry didn't believe him. Why would he?

No one had ever said *that* to him before. No one had ever stayed long enough to believe in him. But Bob believed in Larry enough for both of them. And sometimes, that's all it takes.

High school flew by for Larry, but one thing remained steady—the presence of Uncle Bob. Now, Bob had his own family, his own life, his own responsibilities, but that never changed the way he showed up for Larry. He was the same unwavering force he had always been. A man Larry could count on. A man Larry admired. A man Larry wished he could call *"Dad."*

It wasn't something they talked about. It was just something Larry felt. Deeply.

So when a guest speaker at his high school casually mentioned *college*, the idea stuck—not because it was something Larry had ever seriously considered, but because, for the first time, he wondered if maybe he was capable of more. It wasn't a dream he had. It wasn't even something he dared to say out loud at first.

But he mentioned it to Uncle Bob. Hesitantly. Half-expecting a laugh, a dismissive wave of the hand, or worse—a look that said, "Kid, that's not for you."

Instead, Uncle Bob did what Uncle Bob always did. He looked Larry dead in the eye, steady as ever, and said four words that would change his life: "You can do it."

Field Lessons

College wasn't destiny for Larry. It wasn't a given. It was a question. But Uncle Bob convinced him to try, so he enrolled at the University of Maine at Machias.

What followed was the busiest chapter of his life.

He worked nearly ninety hours a week—motel night shifts, Helen's Restaurant, odd jobs, and the brutal seasonal labor that defined Downeast Maine: raking blueberries. Raking wasn't a side job—it was survival. It paid bills. It built his back. It sharpened his discipline.

And it introduced him to Maine's toughest classroom.

If you've never raked wild blueberries in Downeast Maine, let me paint the picture for you. This isn't a casual summer job. It's not kids standing around with baskets, leisurely picking berries in the soft sunshine. It's a backbreaking, sweat-drenched, hands-bleeding kind of work—the kind that separates the tough from the soft in a matter of hours.

Picture this: You wake up before dawn because the heat of the midday sun will bake you alive. You grab your rake—a heavy metal tool with long tines and a bucket attached—and you hit the barrens. Not *fields*. Not *orchards*. *Barrens*. Because that's what the land looks like—low, scraggly, endless patches of wild blueberries growing out of rocky, unforgiving soil.

Then, you get low. Real low. You crouch, you bend, you drag, you sweat. Over and over for hours, you pull the rake through the thick, stubborn bushes, scraping up every last berry. Your hands get torn up from the stems. Your lower back? It feels like someone's been swinging a sledgehammer at it by noon. The sun beats down, the dirt and sweat mix into a film on your skin, and your arms burn from the repetitive motion. And then you look up and see that you've barely made a dent. Because the barrens? They stretch *forever*.

I learned everything I know about the barrens in a single weekend with my wife's grandfather, Hovey "Pup" Hall. He was one of the best men I've ever met—steady, humble, and as Maine as the soil itself. More than that, he was a true blueberry man, raised on Bell Hill in Whiting, raking alongside his family on the old Halls-Mills land. If anyone understood the barrens—how they work, what they mean, and why they matter—it was Pup. Working alongside Pup, I only raked enough for a couple of blueberry pies, but that was enough for me.

In Downeast Maine, raking blueberries is more than just brutal labor. It's a test. It's the kind of work that earns respect—the kind that proves you can gut it out when things get hard. And it doesn't just test your body—it tests your mind, too. Because when you're out there, with your hands blistering, your back on fire, and miles left to go, you have two choices: Quit. Or keep raking.

Downeast Mainers—Larry's people—are some of the hardest-working folks you'll find in this country. (I'd put money on that.) The people of Downeast Maine are a special breed of hard workers, and if you're from there . . . you don't quit. Period.

A real Downeaster would never complain but let me tell you something about raking blueberries. It's not just hard—it's *merciless.* It's a job you pray to outgrow. A job that kicks your butt every single day and dares you to come back for more. And yet, for folks in Downeast Maine, it's also a *rite of passage*, a *test of grit* that separates the ones who can grind from the ones who quit.

No matter how hard it got, Larry kept raking.

And I believe that that's part of why he made it in banking and in life. Larry wasn't just out there raking blueberries—he was building the *work ethic* that would define the rest of his life. In fact, it was that very grueling work in the barrens that got him noticed.

Larry was out in the field, body aching, sweat drenched, the sun relentless.

Then came *the voice*. A gruff, unmistakable shout from the left edge of the field.

"Hey! If you ever want a job at the bank, come see me."

Larry straightened up, wiped his forehead, and squinted toward the voice. It was coming from Ed.

If you were from Downeast Maine, you didn't need a last name to know who Ed was. Ed Hennessey—President of Machias Savings Bank. The guy who called the shots in a place where "corporate" wasn't really a thing. If there was a king of banking in all of Eastern Maine, Ed easily sported the crown.

Larry went back to work, but Ed's bold voice lingered. The offer sat in his gut like a weight. He wasn't sure if it was opportunity knocking, or just some strange joke. *Banking? Him?* It was easy to doubt himself. Heck, easier to just keep his head down and keep raking, doing what he knew. But then, in the back of his mind, came another voice. One he knew well.

"You can do it."

He heard it plain as day. Uncle Bob's words landing in his heart—loud yet steady, like a whirring helicopter settling in an open field.

And on Monday morning, Larry was at the bank.

One Condition

It was interview day.

Larry *knew* kitchens. He *knew* the scalding sting of dishwater at Helen's Restaurant, the rhythmic scrape of plates, the clatter of silverware tossed into tubs. He *knew* the barrens too—the hard, dusty stretch of land where he raked blueberries under a cruel sun, his sweat-soaked shirt clinging to him like a second and thicker skin. Even the tight corridors of universities, packed with egos, cliques, and the unspoken rules of who's in and who's not. He *knew* that world as well.

But this was foreign soil.

Here in Ed's office. Like a fish out of water.

Ed was ready to hire him. But he wasn't about to just hand him the job.

"I'll hire you," Ed said, "on one condition."

Larry leaned *back*. Ed leaned *forward* and never blinked.

"You *have to* finish your degree."

If Ed had looked closer at Larry's transcript, he might have hesitated even more. Because Larry Barker wasn't just a *late bloomer* in college. He was a stop-and-starter, a detour-taker, a maybe-next-semester guy. His journey to a degree wasn't a straight shot. It wasn't even a winding road. It was an absolute maze.

Larry went back to school to finish what he'd started and launched into the gig at the bank at the same time. No easing in, no adjustment period. If Larry thought Ed's offer meant a smooth ride, he learned fast—there's no elevator to the top. His first job? Collections Department.

It might be the most thankless job in *all of banking.* Heck, maybe the most thankless job in *all of jobs!* It wasn't handing out loans or shaking hands in a polished office. It was knocking on doors. Making the calls no one wanted to answer. Being the guy nobody wanted to hear from. It meant listening to every excuse in the book. Getting hung up on. Getting cussed out by people who felt cornered. It was brutal. It was relentless. It was *real.*

And Larry did it. Every day. Showed up, worked through the discomfort, figured it out. Because that's what separates people.

Larry wasn't a suit-and-tie guy. He wasn't some polished finance prodigy with a crisp diploma and a well-rehearsed elevator pitch. He was a worker. A guy who *executed.* And just because he swapped a blueberry rake for a desk and a phone didn't mean the work stopped.

The Drop

One day, the sitting Senior Commercial Lender at Machias Savings Bank walked out. Just like that. No notice. No transition plan. No months-long search for the perfect replacement. He just up and left—off to chase what he thought were greener pastures. (But you know what they say about greener grass? It still needs mowing.)

Nevertheless, he left Ed Hennessey high and dry. But Ed didn't panic. He didn't scramble. He didn't call a committee meeting to *assess next steps.* He just exhaled through his nose, nodded once, and moved to Plan B. Plan Barker.

Ed walked into collections, dropped a thick stack of files onto Larry's desk, and said, "These are yours now. Don't mess it up, kid."

No welcome speech. No roadmap. No time to ease in. Just sink or swim. Larry had been swimming at Machias Savings Bank in collections for seven years now, and he didn't hesitate.

He executed. He put his head down and got to work. Longer hours. Later nights. Learning everything he could. He wasn't just learning *how* to lend. He was learning *why* the right deals get made and *why* the wrong ones sink businesses. And when Ed threw down a challenge, Larry didn't just meet it—he crushed it.

The twist in all this?

He was still in the fields.

He was still out raking blueberries on the side to make extra money for him and his wife, Terri.

"Yeah, I never completely stopped raking," he said to me during our interview, casual as ever. Like I should've already known. Like it was obvious. "It was always a way I knew I could make money. And Terri and I *really* needed money sometimes."

I had to sit with that. Let it land. This man had a career—a real, demanding, respectable job. And when it was time to step away, to rest, to breathe? He didn't. (And neither did Terri.)

While other people were clocking out, they were clocking *back in.*

While others were unwinding, they were *digging in deeper.*

While others were living for the weekend, they were *working through it.*

The Difference

Eventually, Larry wanted to work smarter—not just harder. He was learning about business, debt financing, and investment through the bank and figured that he'd use his new knowledge to make his blueberry work more manageable—maybe even more lucrative. When he'd saved enough, he bought a blueberry harvester.

Now, if you've never seen a blueberry harvester, *picture this:* a rugged, no-frills machine built for one thing—clearing wild blueberry fields with zero hesitation. It barrels forward, shakes loose what's ripe, leaves the rest, and never looks back. Like a focused team leader, it doesn't waste energy or overthink—it just gets the job done, clean and relentless. The best ones? They don't stop until the field is bare.

That harvester was supposed to be Larry's way of stepping back. The plan? Hire a couple folks to run it so he could finally catch a break. Not a beach-and-margarita break—just trading two grueling jobs for one. He'd use the extra time to push for real progress at the bank, maybe even earn a promotion and a raise. The timing couldn't have been better.

Terri was due to birth their daughter just before harvest. Larry was prepared. He was ready. He had the berry harvesting machine, he had hired the two-person crew needed to run it. For once, he was going to have *time*—a rare chance to be home, to bond with his wife and newborn, to start this new chapter as a family.

Until *two days* before Terri had the baby.

When one part of the two-person team he'd hired quit.

But just like Ed Hennessey when his Senior Commercial Lender walked out unexpectedly, Larry didn't blink. He chose Plan B. Plan Barker.

He took over the harvesting himself, and every second in that harvester was a second stolen from the first days of his newborn daughter's life. Every pass across that field felt like a quiet goodbye to moments he'd never get back. He *should have* been home. He *wanted* to be home.

He worked. He executed. Missing *firsts* he'd never have a chance to see again.

From Blueberries to Boardrooms: The Relentless Climb

That harvester wasn't just a machine—it was a lesson. A grinding, relentless, no-excuses teacher that burned one truth into Larry's bones: *success belongs to those who work, and those that refuse to stop.* So when his boots eventually left the blueberry fields and stepped into banking with more permanence, he carried that same mindset with him.

Thirteen years. That's how long Larry Barker spent in commercial lending—not coasting, not collecting paychecks, but grinding.

If you think it was a cushy gig, *think again.* This was the late 1990s and early 2000s—a time when Machias Savings Bank was growing, and expectations weren't just high, they were sky-high.

Every morning, 6 AM. Larry was at his desk. Not because he had to be. But because that was the standard. For ten years straight, Larry lived by one simple principle: "I was interviewing for my next role every single day."

It paid off.

In 2011, Barker took the reins as President of Machias Savings Bank.

At the time, the bank sat at $950 million in assets—respectable, steady. Today? More than $2.6 billion. That kind of growth doesn't happen by accident. It doesn't happen by playing it safe. And it sure as heck doesn't happen without *great leadership*.

"When I became CEO, I told our team: We're not here to prove ourselves," Larry said. "We're here to improve ourselves."

He has certainly improved himself, which has led to the improvement of his team and organization. And while he won't give you some polished speech about himself, the truth is written all over the way he leads. His leadership isn't built on flashy strategies, corporate jargon, or the latest executive trends. It's built on *three things*. Three unshakable, undeniable pillars.

1. Work Ethic

He *still* outworks the next person. *Period.*

Ask *anyone* at MSB headquarters, and they'll tell you, "No one outworks Larry Barker." I've heard renditions of that line at least half a dozen times from different leaders at the MSB corporate offices. Seasoned bankers—people who've seen it all—are straight-up baffled by the man's engine.

The big title didn't slow him down. The corner office didn't make him comfortable. He still grinds like he's got something to prove—like he's one bad quarter away from losing his seat at the table. But let's be real. At this point, he's not fighting for a seat at the table. He *designed* the table, *built* the table, then *set* the table. And he still shows up at it like he's the underdog.

2. Relationships

He built trust where it *actually* matters—with business owners, employees, and the community. Not through press releases. Not through PR campaigns. Through real conversations, real commitment, and showing up when it counts.

3. Resilience

The financial crisis? He led through it.

The COVID era? He navigated it.

Business Challenges? He doesn't flinch. Doesn't panic. Doesn't crumble. He keeps moving forward, keeps solving problems, keeps finding a way.

Now, he won't tell you all this. He'll just nod toward his team. But if you really look—if you listen between the words—you'll find the truth: Larry Barker built something that lasts. And he did it the only way he knows how—by *showing up, working hard,* and *putting his people first.* Some CEOs chase numbers. Larry chases impact. And impact? It's not rocket science. But when you do it right, it's rocket fuel. That's how you get to the moon.

Legacy

Larry never set out to be CEO. He set out to be excellent. And that's the difference. During our interview, he shared with me the five key lessons he carries with him today. Lessons he has a strong desire to pass on to the youth and to emerging leaders, not just at MSB, but across the globe.

1. Treat people with respect. Every person, every role, every time.
2. Hard work wins. Not sometimes—always.
3. Success isn't about avoiding struggle. It's about embracing it, learning from it, and moving forward.
4. The best leaders don't climb alone. They bring people with them.

And perhaps the most powerful takeaway:

5. "Someone once told me I'd never be a CEO because I was too nice. Turns out, being kind is a pretty good strategy."

Larry Barker didn't inherit his CEO position at Machias Savings Bank. He earned every inch of it.

This is the essence of MADE leadership—an unwavering commitment to serve, to step up when others hesitate, to do what's right simply because it must be done. A MADE leader leads not for accolades or personal gain, but out of a deep sense of duty, responsibility, and purpose. They understand that leadership isn't about position—it's about presence. It's about showing up, lifting others, and making an impact where it matters most.

Because that's how you win for real.

That's how you win by 100.

13

It's Time to Be MADE

So, how do you lead? And not just in your job, but in your life?

When the hard choices show up, do you step forward, or do you shrink back? Do you set the standard, or do you wait to see what everyone else will tolerate? Do you hold yourself accountable, or do you let yourself off the hook when things get uncomfortable?

We don't need a title to lead. We don't need permission. We don't need another meeting, another pep talk, and definitely not another excuse. What we need is to take a long, hard look in the mirror and ask ourselves: *Am I leading the way I should be? Or am I just getting by?*

BMR, Pastor Rae, Larry Barker, and others we've met in these pages don't lead because it's easy. They lead the way they do because they've been MADE. They've learned to operate with purpose, with integrity, and with an unshakable commitment to doing things the right way. And if you want to be a great leader, one who wins by a hundred without walking all over the backs of others, you owe it to yourself to do the same.

To be MADE is to lead with the *right* mindset—for the *right* reasons. It means demanding excellence from yourself without stepping on people to get there. It means chasing success, but never at the expense of your values. It means *winning* but refusing to compromise your integrity to do it.

MADE leaders show up *every time, all the time*. They do the work when no one is watching. They do the hard thing because it's hard. They push forward, even when it's uncomfortable, because they refuse to live a life of mediocrity. They want to win! And they know there's nothing wrong with owning that desire.

I hate to say it, but most people won't do the work. They'll settle. They'll nod along, feel inspired, and swear they're ready to change—only to slide right back into the same patterns.

Slippage, in my experience, is the quiet killer of every breakthrough.

I write this book *knowing* that most of the people who read it will get fired up for a few weeks (or days), and then, just like that, they'll slide back to where they were before engaging the MADE framework. They'll let life get in the way. They'll find excuses. They'll tell themselves that good enough is going to have to be just fine.

Don't let that be you.

No Spotlight, Just Sweat

Execution is where the rubber meets the road. It's not about inspiration or intention—it's about action. Without execution, your goals are just dreams you casually mention, hoping someone will validate them. With execution, they become tangible achievements that redefine your life.

Nobody cares about what you want to do.

Results come only from what you actually do.

I know this because I've lived it. When I started writing this book two years ago, it was just another idea, one of the countless concepts swirling in my head. MADE, the concept itself was born in one of those moments—in the shower, of all places.

Earlier that day, I'd been interviewed by an HR magazine about my role as a Senior Partner in our Holloway Group Professional Development Firm and my work as an executive coach. I answered her questions about how I do what I do, but my response left me unsettled. It felt jumbled and unconvincing. I couldn't let it go. I felt I'd bombed the interview and didn't do the best job explaining myself.

I thought about it all day—through dinner, while putting my kids to bed, even in the shower before calling it a night. And that's when it struck me: people only see the polished presentation of what I do. They never see the process—the "kitchen" where the magic happens.

It's like a restaurant: patrons enjoy the meal, but they're never brought through the kitchen to witness how it's made. In that moment, I knew I needed to better define and share my process—the foundation of everything I do with clients. I needed to give a tour of the kitchen . . . where the magic is made . . . "where the magic is MADE!" I said aloud.

That was the moment the framework clicked.

- **Motivation**: Because without it, nothing moves.
- **Assessment**: Because growth starts with truth.
- **Declaration**: Because unspoken intentions die quiet deaths.
- **Execution**: Because action is the only thing that counts.

MADE wasn't theory, wasn't just something I'd taught. It was survival. It was something I lived.

I can still picture the moment vividly: bursting out of the bathroom, dripping wet, wrapped in a towel, and shouting the concept to Bre as she lay in bed half asleep. "I have an idea . . . No, I have the idea!"

The framework clicked instantly. It wasn't just something I practiced instinctively—it was something I could teach, something that could change lives. But knowing wasn't enough; I had to do the work to bring it to life.

At the time, my plate wasn't just full—it was overflowing and bending under the weight. I was teaching full-time at Husson University, running my professional development firm, and raising three incredible kids—Grace, Jace, and Jaxon—while showing up for every game, practice, and performance I could.

I was often on the road for work in various cities far from home. My days were packed. My energy was stretched thin. And my motivation? It came and went like New England summer—bright one moment, gone the next.

It would've been easy—real easy—to shelve this book. To call it "bad timing." To let it become just another deferred dream.

But if I was going to write a book about being MADE, I had to live MADE. I had to find my motivation again. I had to assess my habits, my time, my excuses. And I had to declare—out loud and in public—that this book was getting written in 2025. That was it. No turning back. I wasn't about to make promises and not follow through. I wasn't about to look like Boo-Boo the Fool and fall short on my own words.

So that left one thing: Execute.

Execution wasn't easy. I had to gut my schedule and rebuild it from the ground up. I used to tell myself fifteen minutes wasn't enough time to write—so I'd scroll on my phone instead. I had to unlearn that excuse. I had to replace comfort with consistency.

For the past ten months, I've been up at 5:00 AM—writing before the world wakes up. From 5 to 7:30, it's just me, this book, and the grind. Then I shift into dad mode: coffee with Bre, packing lunches, and seeing the kids off to school. And most nights? I'm back at it after 9:00 PM, once the house quiets down—after the dishes, emptying the trash, reading the bedtime stories.

This book wasn't born out of convenience. It was carved out of chaos. And that's the point.

Being MADE doesn't happen in the highlights. It's built in the quiet, gritty, unseen moments—when nobody's watching, and you still choose to show up.

I didn't just write this book.

I became this book.

This process has transformed me. It's shown me what I'm capable of when I lean into discomfort and commit to the grind. It's taught me resilience—the ability to keep going even when I'm tired. It's built my confidence, proving I can achieve big things even in the busiest seasons of life. And it's grown my self-trust, showing me I can keep promises to myself, no matter how hard the road gets.

And I'm not the only one who's lived the grind of execution.

- Cooper could've coasted on raw talent and been great. Instead, he trains with Matt like greatness owes him nothing—and shows up every single day to prove it.
- Zavier tore his meniscus his rookie year with the Colts. An injury that causes many guys to tap out. He doubled down—disciplined rehab, relentless focus—and came back stronger.
- Larry didn't pitch perfect ideas working in Collections. He executed—consistently—until his

results spoke louder than anyone's opinions. And he got called to the front.

These aren't stories of luck. They're stories of grit. Because execution isn't about big moments or grand gestures. It's about doing the work when nobody's around to see. It's about nailing the fundamentals—again, and again, and again—until results are undeniable. It's ABCD: focusing your Attention on a goal, doubling-down on Belief, then Delivering when given the Chance.

Execution doesn't play favorites. It rewards resilience and grit, plain and simple. When you commit to consistent execution, the rewards are undeniable: losing weight, building savings, earning a degree, landing a promotion, starting a business. These aren't fantasies; they're the visible outcomes of showing up daily. Small wins may seem insignificant in the moment, but they stack up. Before you know it, you're standing in a life you once thought was out of reach.

MAD Isn't MADE

If you've made it this far through MADE, here's what you've done:

You got Motivated.

Something sparked in you. Maybe pain. Maybe purpose. Maybe a mix of both. But something inside said, "I want to be better."

You did an Assessment.

You told yourself the truth. You looked in the mirror and admitted the gaps, the blind spots, the cracks in your character that you'd managed to ignore—but were hard to live with.

Then you made a Declaration.

Out loud. You told your team, your family, your circle: "Here's where I'm going. Who I'll become. Hold me to it."

One of the questions I most often get asked about the MADE system is:

What if I fail to Execute?

I get why it's asked. Once you say something out loud, once you make a declaration—like I did around writing this book—the stakes feel real. The fear of failing in public, of letting people down, of letting *yourself* down—that's heavy.

So, what if you stopped right there?

What if you didn't do what you said you were going to do.

And didn't become who you said you were becoming.

You'd be MAD!

But you wouldn't be MADE.

Simply put:

Motivation + Assessment + Declaration + Execution equals MADE. And MADE = Transformation.

Motivation + Assessment + Declaration – Execution equals MAD. While MAD = Frustration.

When I work with organizations and teams, one of my core responsibilities is identifying who *executes and who doesn't*. Not based on charisma. Not based on how passionate someone sounds in a meeting. Not based on the best-laid declarations. But based solely on whether they *actually* do the work they said they would do.

Because failure to execute isn't just a dropped task.

It's a dropped standard.

It's a ripple effect.

It's broken trust.

It's wasted potential.

It's a credibility leak.

Truthfully, a broken promise from a leader is just betrayal (maybe with better PR).

So, get out there and execute before your brand becomes your excuse.

Winning – For Real

If you'd asked me when I first knew I wanted to be a winner, I would've told you I was born that way. And I wouldn't be lying – at least not on the surface.

My first memorable win? Third-grade spelling bee. Ms. Susan Curlee's class at George Watts Elementary. I can still hear her voice when I nailed it: "I-M-P-O-R-T-A-N-T. Important." She smiled. I beamed. I was eight years old and floating.

I'd had a crush on Ms. Curlee since the second week of school. She was kind and encouraging – easily the kindest person I'd ever met. The attention she gave me that day, when I won, made me feel important—and not just because that was the winning word. The way she looked at me, smiled, clapped—it stuck. That spelling bee didn't just win me a ribbon. It won her attention. That was the moment I started chasing wins.

Later that same school year came Field Day—the best day of the year. No classes, just competition. Hula-hooping, racing, jumping rope, tossing rings, getting soaked in water balloon fights. It was noisy, messy, and a blast.

Three events. Three ribbons. I ran through the front door and threw them on the kitchen counter, puffed-up and ready to be celebrated. Hugs. High fives. Even my cousin Nilsa from New York handed me two bucks and called me "champ." That kind of approval sticks.

I was ten feet tall . . . until my big brother Derrick got home.

I had taped all my ribbons to our bedroom wall. Derrick wasn't impressed. "Blue ones can stay," he said, "but, bruh, not that red one." He flicked my red ribbon like it was lint. That little flick hit me harder than I expected.

He read the back: "50 Yard Dash." In that moment I remembered Mike-Mike, the skinny kid who beat me by a foot. Mike-Mike won. And I hated him for about three seconds when that memory came back, because he'd cost me Derrick's nod.

Derrick glanced at one of the blue ribbons. "Tug o' War," he said. Team sport. No MVP in Tug o' War. That left me one ribbon I could defend: my solo blue. Third-grade Frisbee Toss Champion. It wasn't much, but it was mine.

On that day, I began my disdain for second place. I learned that in life, there are blue ribbons and red ribbons. Get the blue ones. They're I-M-P-O-R-T-A-N-T.

In middle school, blue ribbons became cardstock certificates. In high school, they were trophies. By ninth grade Derrick had gone off to boot camp, and the walls were mine to fill however I saw fit. Now my room had trophies—chorus, basketball, track and field—anything I could enter and win. Winning made me feel seen. And I wanted to be seen.

Trophies didn't need a wall. They announced themselves. Anyone who walked into my room could see it. I was a winner. And deep down I needed them to know it.

When I left for college, my parents moved to a smaller home. Somewhere in that move, all my trophies disappeared. Gone. When I found out during Thanksgiving break, I wasn't even mad. My apathy surprised me.

I thought back on those wins. They were fun memories: cute, confidence-builders. But if I'd lost any of those competitions, what would it have cost me? Nothing. No doors would've closed. No reputation would've suffered. Those wins gave me confidence but not cost. And when there's no cost, there's no real value. Confidence without consequence is just noise.

The fact that I wasn't even mad about the lost box of trophies said something. It showed I was starting to understand: Real winning doesn't live on a shelf. It lives in what it costs you. Real winning puts something on the line. Real winning demands more than skill. It demands skin in the game.

I used to be competitive just to be competitive, like my son Jaxon is now, charging after every ball in his second-grade soccer league, asking me, "Did we win?" If you've been with me since the beginning of this book, you've already met him on that field. That hunger in his voice? I know it well.

But competition without purpose is just ego management. If applause is the prize, you didn't win. You just got clapped for. Real winning starts when losing really costs you something.

And up until eighteen years ago, I really had nothing to lose.

Then came Grace-Lyn—my firstborn. You haven't "met" her in these pages until now, but she's been behind every story you've read. When she took her first breath, it felt like I took mine.

Becoming a father, especially to a little girl, shifts everything. I held her in my arms, and something clicked. Life snapped into focus. My choices weren't just mine anymore. My losses wouldn't just hurt me. They'd hurt her, too.

Suddenly, winning wasn't optional. It was required. She was the first person I ever wanted to win by 100 for. She made losing unacceptable. She gave me a real why, and over time that why grew with the births of my sons, Jace and Jaxon.

Before Grace-Lyn, I liked to win. After her, I had to win. Not just to feel proud, but to protect her future. To make sure she never paid the price for my failure.

Her birth created urgency in me. Eventually, it birthed something bigger: MADE. I didn't know the framework yet, but it was already alive in me.

- **Motivation**: My wife and kids. My reasons. My why.
- **Assessment**: The honest-mirror conversations I stopped avoiding.
- **Declaration**: The promise I made to be the man they all needed.
- **Execution**: The daily grind to become that man. No days off. No finish line.

MADE wasn't born out of ambition. It was forged in responsibility. It came from love. It rose from the refusal to fail the people who needed me.

That day at Bangor Savings Bank when I was just an intern, BMR helped wake me up to the idea of winning by 100, putting words to the music that had been playing in my mind ever since Grace-Lyn was born. Now, when I watch Grace-Lyn killing it in her life, or Jace making all the right plays on the basketball court, or Jaxon sprinting across a soccer field with that fire in his eyes, I smile because I know one day they'll fully understand. While wanting to win is natural, needing to win for someone who's counting on you—that's transformational.

I believe that moment has come for you, too. The moment when your ego, your excuses, your image no longer matter, because something in your life matters more. When losing is no longer acceptable. When winning—and winning by 100—becomes necessary.

That's when you finally understand that winning isn't about beating others. It's about refusing to fail the ones counting on you. It's about building a life and a legacy you don't have to apologize for. It's about knowing you emptied the tank with dignity and respect, just like BMR taught me in that office on day one.

Winners aren't born. They're MADE. And MADE leaders don't chase hollow wins. They keep score the right way. They do the work in the dark. They honor their values in the light and the dark. And then, when the moment comes, they win by 100 in the ways that matter most.

It's winning time.

Go do the work.

Go be MADE.

And go win by 100 for the people who are counting on you.

Acknowledgements

No one does anything great alone. Not one person.

This book—and the mission behind it—wasn't built in isolation. It was shaped by love, belief, sacrifice, and the boldness of people who stood with me when all I had was conviction and a calling.

To my family—Breanne, Grace, Jace, and Jaxon—thank you. You gave me the space to chase this work when it cost time, sleep, and presence. Breanne—this doesn't happen without you. Your strength, patience, and belief held it all together when I was stretched beyond capacity. My name is on the cover, but your fingerprints are all over every page.

To my parents, Pastor Deborah Holloway and Dr. Johnny Holloway—thank you for the blueprint. You taught me to seek truth, speak truth, and stand firm in wisdom. The principles you raised me on still guide every decision I make.

To the Win By A Hundred core team—Cary Weston, Ron Roth Jr., Kaleb Currier, Greg Newton Brown, and Emma Rose—thank you. You've been steady hands, sharp minds, and loyal hearts. You didn't just help shape the message—you made sure it was honest and accurate.

To the leaders who believed in me early—Wendy Durrah and Bob Montgomery-Rice—thank you. You didn't just bet on the work—you bet on me. That "yes" gave me a runway.

To Larry Barker and Danielle Daley—thank you for doubling down. You told me to go further. You trusted me with your people, and that trust fueled this work more than you know.

To Pastor Bill Rae—A real man. You picked up the pieces of a broken man and listened when I needed it most.

To Dr. Marie Hansen—hands down, the best boss I've ever had. You didn't just nod at my dreams—you helped build them. When I was running on fumes, you stood by me harder than anyone outside my wife ever has.

To the educators who helped sharpen MADE—thank you. Dan Crocker, thank you for being my academic rock. To the Husson MBA faculty, and to Dr. Mike Knupp, Dr. Lee Speronis, and Dr. Rich Fabri—your insight and support gave structure to conviction. You helped turn this from a framework into a force.

Finally, to the organizations I've had the honor to serve—you've never just been clients. You've been co-creators, allies, and in many cases, friends. You let me into your cultures and leadership struggles—and that trust is sacred.

Win By 100 may have my name on the cover—but it carries the voices, belief, and fingerprints of the village that built it.

—TJ

About the Author

Terrence "TJ" Holloway is an executive coach, business strategist, and founder of The Holloway Group, LLC. He has spent over a decade teaching undergraduates and MBA students while coaching top leaders and teams across the U.S. and Canada. Known for his candor, insight, and no-fluff style, he helps leaders gain clarity, build strong cultures, and sustain success.

Made in the USA
Coppell, TX
21 June 2026

82732335R00166